WRITERS OF THE OLD WEST

Volume 18

True Tales of the Old West

by

Charles L. Convis

Watercolor Cover by Mary Anne Convis

PIONEER PRESS, CARSON CITY, NEVADA

Library of Congress Catalog Card Number: 96-68502

ISBN 1-892156-08-3 (Volume)
ISBN 0-9651954-0-6 (Series)

Printed by
KNI, Incorporated
Anaheim, California

CONTENTS

ILLUSTRATIONS

Alvar Nunez Cabeza de Vaca

THE BEGINNING OF AMERICAN LITERATURE

American literature began with Alvar Nunez Cabeza de Vaca publishing his *La Relacion* in 1542. The book described an eight-year ordeal of triumph over obstacles, unmatched outside Greek mythology.

In April, 1528, Cabeza de Vaca and six hundred adventurous Spaniards led by Panfilo de Narvaez, landed on the west coast of Florida to search for fabled cities of gold. As treasurer and high-sheriff, Cabeza de Vaca was one of the leading officers of the expedition.

In early November two homemade boats crashed through the breakers near Galveston Island, dumping Cabeza de Vaca and about eighty companions on to the beach. The other explorers were never heard of again.

The survivors tried in vain to re-launch their boats. They lost their clothing, weapons, food, and supplies in the attempt. Four volunteers set out for Mexico by land. They were never heard from again. The rest were stranded, naked and defenseless, on a strange and forbidding coast.

Fortunately the native Karankawa Indians were peaceful. They showed the strange men from an unknown land how to dig roots, make fishing gear, and capture animals for skins.

Only fifteen men survived the first winter of cold, starvation and disease. A few of the Spaniards ate the flesh of their dead companions. Indians, shocked at such incomprehensible conduct, enslaved them all.

For the next six years, the Spaniards — their numbers decreasing each year — were bought, sold and traded among all the coastal tribes. Finally, only Cabeza de Vaca, Andres Dorantes, Alonzo del Castillo, and Estevanico, Dorantes' Moorish slave, were left.

These four, the only survivors of Narvaez' expedition, escaped their Indian captors. Their two-year journey across present Texas, New Mexico and Arizona and down the west coast of Mexico to Culiacan was acclaimed as one of the world's most incredible feats of courage and fortitude.

The first tribe they met as they moved west across Texas thought Castillo was a medicine man. Some Indians, saying they had headaches, asked Castillo to cure them. He made the sign of the cross and commended the sick men to God. Their pain stopped.

After a short visit, the tribe escorted the fugitives on to the next tribe west. This time the new Indians presented a patient who had no pulse and whose eyes were rolled back in his head. Castillo, a timid healer, declined the challenge. Cabeza de Vaca stepped forward and "supplicated the Lord as fervently as I could, that He would give health to the sick man and all that had need of it." Many were cured that day, including the one with no pulse.

As they struggled westward into the unknown, the Spaniards prayed constantly for the power to heal, realizing it was their only passport to safety. After eight months with the second tribe, they moved on. As each tribe escorted them on to the next, their reputations as miraculous children of the sun grew.

At one tribe, probably in present West Texas, Cabeza de Vaca was asked to cure an Indian who suffered from an old arrow wound. By careful probing he realized the arrow point was lodged in a cartilage near the heart. He opened the man's chest with a knife and removed the arrowhead. He sewed up the surgical wound with thread made from animal hair. The tribe celebrated for days. They sent messengers into the back country so others of their tribe could come and view the miracle of the stranger's skill.

Cabeza de Vaca was a sympathetic observer of the Indians. Even when enslaved by the Karankawas, he noted their remarkable love for their children. The death of a son was followed by a year of communal mourning. Twice each day the lost child was remembered with wailings of sorrow.

In his descriptions of Indian social customs, he mentioned their acceptance of homosexuality, which he called a diabolical practice, and their use of a mind-altering substance which they smoked. He was the first writer to describe the American bison.

In 1536, eight years after they had landed on the Florida coast, the four survivors reached other Spaniards in Mexico. Several days passed before they could wear clothing confortably and sleep off the ground. Cabeza de Vaca sailed back to Spain, where he published his account of the journey. The others stayed in America.

Cabeza de Vaca's book was the first European account of life in the Western Hemisphere. An outstanding epic of endurance and survival, it also described the writer's spiritual journey beyond the boundaries of his familiar world.

Suggested reading: Buckingham Smith, *Relation of Alvar Nunez Cabeza de Vaca* (Ann Arbor: Univ. Microfilms, 1966).

The Account: Alonso Nunez Cabeza de Vaca's Relacion

IMAGINATIVE WRITER

W hen George Catlin gave up law practice to record a disappearing way of life, he did more than paint. He devoted his life to "describing the living manners, customs and character of a people who were rapidly passing away from the face of the earth — a dying nation who had no historians or biographers of their own."

Catlin's careful attention to detail made his reputation as the best of the early painters of Indians. He also made many notes of what he saw and heard. But some of his writing should be taken with a grain of salt.

Catlin's vivid imagination, developed during boyhood reading about Indians, is best shown in his account of the burial of Omaha Chief Black Bird. Black Bird was buried on a high bluff overlooking the Missouri River, so he could "watch the French trappers as they passed up and down."

Catlin visited Black Bird's grave in 1832 while returning from the Mandan villages. He had stopped a few miles upstream to spend two days at the grave of Sergeant Charles Floyd, who died in 1804 while on the Lewis and Clark expedition.

Catlin was already in an expansive mood. He said the voyage down from the Teton River was the most delightful of the whole tour. "A thousand thousand velvet-covered hills were tossing and leaping down the river's edge, as if to grace its shores. All the breathings of the day are hushed, and nought but the soft notes of the dove can be heard; or the still softer and more plaintive notes of the wolf, who sneaks through these scenes of enchantment and mournfully howls as if lonesome, lost in the stillness about him."

Catlin sat at Floyd's grave and contemplated in solitude. "Nothing but the soft-breathing winds was heard to break the stillness of the scene. No chirping bird or sound of cricket, nor soaring eagle's scream were interposed between God and man. Nothing to check man's whole surrender of his soul to his Creator."

Without doubt, Black Bird was buried where Catlin had stopped. His grave, like Floyd's, was marked with a cedar post. Catlin said Black Bird wanted to be buried on the back of his favorite war horse. As a leading Omaha chief, Black Bird could have been buried on the back of any horse on any bluff he chose.

Catlin may have surrendered more than he was aware of as he contemplated in his expansive mood. He wrote that Black Bird's horse was buried alive.

Catlin wrote: "The noble steed was led to the top of the grass-covered hill, and, with great pomp and ceremony, in the presence of the whole nation, several fur traders and the Indian agent, Black Bird's body was placed on the horse's back."

Black Bird was buried holding his bow with his quiver slung over his back. The scalps Black Bird had taken during his many battles were hung on the horse's bridle. At the last moment, the warriors placed on the chief's head his beautiful headdress of war eagle plumes. Finally, "every warrior of the band painted the palm and fingers of his right hand with vermillion, which was stamped and perfectly impressed on the milk-white sides of his devoted horse."

By now the devoted horse had demonstrated remarkable patience, but the best was yet to come: The Indians filled the grave with dirt. Catlin said they "started around the feet and legs of the horse, and gradually laid up turfs to its sides; and at last, over the back and head of the unsuspecting animal, and last of all over the head and even the eagle plumes of its valiant rider, where all together have smouldered and remained undisturbed to the present day."

Catlin also wrote an interesting account of the war training of young Mandan boys. He said several hundred of the boys would be divided into two companies, each led by an experienced warrior. Each boy carried a small bow, harmless arrows made from grass, and a small wooden knife belted to his naked body. A small tuft of grass was attached to each boy's hair as a pretend scalp.

The two companies were brought together as if in battle. The boys shot their own arrows and dodged others. When a boy was struck in a vital part of his body, he was required to fall. Then his adversary rushed up, drew his play knife, and took the grass scalp.

The sham fights were followed by educational comments from the watching warriors. A sham scalp dance ended the exercise. Very likely, Catlin's account of the training was accurate. He made a detailed drawing of the exercise. But considering his story about the burial of Black Bird and his live horse, how could one ever be sure?

Suggested reading: George Catlin, *North American Indians* (Edinburgh: John Grant, 1926).

North American Indians

EARLY WAR CORRESPONDENT

George Wilkins Kendall, descended from Englishmen and Welshmen who had come to the colonies before the revolution, was working on Horace Greeley's New York newspaper in 1833 when he ran a borrowed fifteen dollars up to seven hundred in a poker game. He promptly quit his job and headed for New Orleans to start his own paper. Jobs on Washington and Alabama newspapers delayed him, and he started the *New Orleans Picayune* in January, 1837. It was the city's first inexpensive newspaper.

At that time foreign coins were legal tender in the United States. The smallest coin in circulation was the Spanish "picayon." Worth six and one-fourth cents, it gave the new newspaper its name and its price.

Kendall, a restless adventurer and searcher for news, made several circulation-developing trips into the Republic of Texas. In 1841 Mirabeau Lamar, hero at San Jacinto and now Texas' second president, claimed the Rio Grande as his country's western boundary. He proposed an expedition to Santa Fe, located on the Texas side of that boundary. If the area's residents accepted Texas sovereignty, the rich Santa Fe trade would cross Texas to Texas ports. Former president Sam Houston thought the venture foolish, but Lamar went ahead.

The expedition was expected to last four months. Kendall thought it a great opportunity to satisfy his wanderlust and to obtain a supply of interesting stories for his newspaper. He arrived in Houston on May 18, 1841, and rode on to Austin to join. He reported for duty with a pair of pistols, a Bowie knife, a rifle, a riding horse, and a pack mule.

One night, shortly before the expedition's departure, Kendall led a group from their Austin hotel to the Colorado River for a swim. It was pitch dark, he was unfamiliar with the route, and he walked off a cliff into a long fall where he severely crushed his ankle. Glad to have a reporter on the expedition, the Texian leaders now provided Kendall with a comfortable wagon.

The expedition became a tragic fiasco. Hostile Indians killed some; Mexican soldiers captured the rest. Some men died on the march to Mexican prisons; others were executed by their captors.

Kendall's vivid descriptions of Indian villages, prairie dog cities, and riding through a large gathering of rattlesnakes, and his accounts of such incidents as cold-blooded executions and how it feels to be starving to death provided many stories. He had a valid passport for travel into Mexico, but it was not recognized by his captors. Finally he was released in April, 1842, after seven months of illegal confinement.

Even then Kendall was not eager to leave the country. He stayed another month to collect material for stories about the local inhabitants. He bought gifts and took them to companions, still in prison. Once he met a young girl in the street who seemed vaguely familiar. When she saw Kendall, she threw her arms around him, and "embraced me with as much cordiality as though I had been one of her dearest friends." Mexicans passing in the street paid no attention to the exuberant greetings, but it took Kendall a little while to realize that the girl was a sister of one of the men who had guarded them in prison. She had often brought her brother his meal, sometimes carrying extra food for the prisoners.

Another story he mentioned was his difficulty in sleeping after his release. For seven months on a two-thousand-mile painful march, where he had seen comrades inhumanely butchered or die from disease, he had slept well except when his own illness or freezing weather interfered. Yet, upon release it seemed that the quiet comfort he now enjoyed kept him awake. He missed the earthen and stone floors, the clanking of chains, the groans of fellow prisoners.

Kendall's stories made the *Picayune* New Orleans' greatest newspaper. Published in book form in London in 1845, the stories became an international best seller. They helped explain the animosity Texians had toward Mexico, which found expression in the United States war against Mexico.

Kendall served in that war as the modern world's first war correspondent. He was mentioned for valor, was wounded, and he even captured an enemy battle flag. He established a pony express to speed his dispatches from the battlefield to his newspaper. New York papers often quoted the *Picayune* as the source of their war news.

For a quarter of a century Kendall was considered Texas' greatest press agent. He retired to raise sheep in the Texas Hill Country which he had first seen (and fallen from) on the expedition to Mexico. His sheep ranch took up most of Kendall County, named for a great newspaperman by a grateful state.

✻ Suggested reading: Fayette Copeland, *Kendall of the Picayune* (Norman: Univ. of Oklahoma Press, 1943).

THEY TOLD OF WESTERN TRAILS

Frances Parkman's Harvard classmates said he had Indians on the brain. He loved hunting and trapping, and he spent college vacations canoeing in New England mountains. After he graduated from both Harvard College and Harvard Law School, he went west to learn more about Indians.

Accompanied by friend and cousin Quincy Adams Shaw, Parkman reached St. Louis in April, 1846. He had letters of introduction to wealthy fur traders and plenty of money to buy equipment. At the traders' suggestion he hired mountain man Henry Chatillon as guide.

After buying livestock and equipment in Westport and hiring a muleteer, Parkman met a Britisher, Captain William Chandler, who had planned a hunting trip to the Rocky Mountains with his brother. Although Chandler had an experienced guide, a muleteer, and two French-Canadian hunters, he thought his party too small to be safe from Indians. Parkman agreed to join him.

Parkman bought a fifteen-pound rifle and two pistols. He carried a sheath knife in his belt. Shaw carried a double-barreled shotgun. Astride his horse, Pontiac, Parkman looked approvingly over his outfit. Emigrants, whom Parkman called "Kentucky Fellows," were camped nearby.

Parkman wrote: "They were in great confusion, holding meetings, passing resolutions, and drawing up regulations, but unable to unite in the choice of leaders to conduct them across the prairie." He thought his own four-man outfit ready for any frontier adventure, particularly with the six-man Chandler group as allies.

Westport was scarcely out of sight when Parkman's cart sunk to its axle while crossing a gully. By the time they got it out, the four men looked as bedraggled and muddy as any of the emigrants Parkman had disdained.

They caught up with their British friends at Fort Leavenworth. Parkman had a letter of introduction to Stephen Watts Kearny, the post commander. They enjoyed the colonel's hospitality while Chandler talked of past steeplechases and future buffalo hunts. They rode over to the Kickapoo village to call on a trader. The trader's Creole wife set out iced water and an excellent claret. The taste of luxury at the edge of civilization sharpened the drama of the impending journey.

The next day the combined groups made a spectacular departure. Chandler's guide was sure he knew the way across the ocean of grass to the Oregon trail. They were surprised, after riding a couple of hours, to see a cluster of buildings ahead. Drawing nearer, they realized that their horses and mules, bought in the Westport area, had taken them in a circle back to the Kickapoo village they had started from with such fanfare and optimism.

The kindly trader pointed out the right way to go and reminded them that the sun rose in the east and set in the west.

They came upon an abandoned cow after they had been without game for some time, so the Englishmen decided to rope her and add her to their diet. They were unable to rope the animal, so a frustrated Chandler shot her through the stomach. Unable to run any more, the cow followed along painfully. Then the travelers saw an object through the trees that looked like a covered wagon.

"Let that cow drop back." Chandler shouted. "I think her owners are up ahead."

The object they had seen turned out to be a large, white rock. That night they butchered the cow, enjoying the addition to their limited bill of fare.

When they reached the Platte River, they met men riding back down the trail. Parkman was thrilled to hear one of them ask: "How are ye, boys? Are ye fer Oregon or Californy?" Now Parkman felt like a genuine emigrant, a real pioneer.

The two groups separated after they crossed the South Platte. Parkman's group rode on to Fort Laramie and then camped for two weeks on the Chugwater before heading back east. During that time Parkman rode to the fort for provisions and news. On one of the nights he was at the fort — June 27 — three other men were there, who would later become famous writers also: Edwin Bryant, at that time traveling with the Donner-Reed party, and J. Quinn Thornton were going west; James Clyman was going east.

These three writers, whose paths crossed Parkman's in an amazing coincidence, became important chroniclers of the Oregon Trail. But Parkman's *The Oregon Trail* became a classic. The other three knew more about the trail and living in the wilds, but Parker's vivid descriptions of the country and the Indians made his book a classic, enjoyed by all.

Parkman, filled more with energy than expertise, didn't travel very far west, but his book did much to alleviate public concern about crossing strange country peopled by Indians. Its contribution to the rush of gold-seeking men three years later was immense.

✗Suggested reading: Frances Parkman, *The Oregon Trail* (Garden City: Doubleday & Co., inc., 1946).

TRAVEL WRITER

Bayard Taylor was a born wanderer. He learned to read at four; his favorites were travel books. After a schooling in literature and language, he became a typesetter on a local newspaper in Chester County, Pennsylvania. He published a small volume of poetry in 1844, when he was nineteen. After walking to Washington to get their passports, he and a cousin sailed to London.

When they returned two years later, Taylor published an account of his travels and experiences. It ran through six editions in its first year, fourteen more in its first decade.

In 1847 Taylor began a lifelong career with the *New York Tribune* and its editor, Horace Greeley. Greeley knew the California Gold Rush was a story his newspaper should cover and Taylor was the best man to write it. He sent Taylor west in June, 1849. Taylor was probably the only Argonaut that year who went to California to observe, rather than to get rich.

Taylor's vivid, accurate writing about California has never been surpassed. He was interested equally in the geography and the people. He wrote this about a trip through the Santa Clara Valley:

"The mountain rose like an island in the sea of air, so far removed from all it overlooked that everything was wrapped in a subtle violet haze, through which the features of the scene seemed grander and more distant than the reality. West of us, range behind range, ran the Coast Mountains, parted by deep, wild valleys, in which we could trace the course of streams, shaded by the pine and the gallant redwood."

Taylor was shocked at the cost of goods and services. He worried that eastern readers would not believe that a lawyer paid $250 monthly rent for a twelve-foot square, six-foot deep cellar office; that street car teamsters got five hundred dollars a month; and that a fifteen-year-old boy won five hundred dollars in a few minutes at a faro table. He told of small children panning dust swept up from the streets and recovering more money in a day than grown men made in a month back east.

Taylor rode a mule to Stockton and on to the mines. He traveled with Lieutenant Edward F. Beale, a messenger who had carried gold discovery news back east the year before. Stockton was a canvas town of a thousand people with twenty-five vessels at anchor. Four months before, it had been one ranch, hidden in the tule marshes.

Taylor reported from the diggings on the Mokelumne River. He covered the actions of the miners' courts. He saw a man whose ears had been cut off for stealing.

Taylor described native Californios as superb horsemen who roped bears with lariats. They could read animals like other men read newspapers. After passing dozens of horses in a day's journey, they could describe each one in detail.

In September Taylor covered California's Constitutional Convention in Monterey. While there, he examined land grant records created under Spanish governments. He accurately predicted the costly litigation that would one day be required to clear titles.

Taylor returned to New York in January 1850. Most of the public's information about the gold rush came from his writing. Later that year, he published his book, *Eldorado*. It was reprinted in both New York and London before the year was out. He dedicated the book to Lieutenant Beale.

Bayard Taylor was one of the most popular and productive writers of his time. He was a poet, an artist, a man of letters, and a student of history. He understood the social and political implications in what he observed. He said he wanted to describe "an incredible epoch, crowded with life and action." He, alone, seemed to understand that "a man, on coming to California, could no more expect to retain his old nature unchanged than he could retain in his lungs the air he had inhaled on the Atlantic shore."

In October, 1850, Taylor married his childhood sweetheart, although they both knew she had tuberculosis. She died within two months. He continued to travel all over the world, and he wrote many more books. He knew Germany better than any American, and President Hayes appointed him minister to that country. He died there in 1878, working on a biography of Goethe.

Taylor sought recognition as a poet and novelist. With a few exceptions, most judge his fiction and poetry mediocre. His non-fiction travel writings, however, were outstanding.

Suggested reading: Bayard Taylor, *Eldorado* (New York: Alfred A. Knopf, 1949).

LETTERS FROM THE MINES

Louise Smith grew up lonely. Orphaned at seven with six brothers and sisters scattered among relatives, she found companionship in books. She reached maturity in the literary culture of Amherst, Massachusetts. She mastered foreign languages and learned to read the flowery, over-drawn prose, stylish for young ladies' literature at the time. But the petite, golden-haired beauty wanted adventure away from New England libraries.

In 1837, when Louise was eighteen, she met Alexander Everett, a prominent scholar and diplomat. Everett, twice her age and already married, fell in love with the girl. The only result of the one-sided affair was a long correspondence in which Everett urged her to become a writer. "If you were to add to the love of reading the habit of writing, you would find a new and inexhaustible source of comfort and satisfaction opening for you," he wrote. Not until Louise died at eighty-six and a packet of Everett's letters were found near her body, did anyone know of the correspondence.

In 1847 Louise, twenty-eight, married Fayette Clappe, a medical student five years younger. Everett never wrote Louise after her marriage. He died a few months later. He had, however, during the ten years of their correspondence, helped her to her first publication.

Two years after their marriage, Louise and Fayette sailed around Cape Horn to San Francisco. A year later they went to the Feather River mines, settling at Rich Bar. When Louise told her San Francisco friends she was following her husband to the mines, they said she should be put in a strait jacket.

"But I'm looking forward to riding a mule to the bottom of the Feather River Canyon," she said. "It's quite deep, you know."

The ride was less pleasant than she expected. Fayette got them lost, near where another couple had been murdered just a few weeks before.

In 1851-52 Louise wrote twenty-three letters to her sister, Mary, back in New England. Signed "Dame Shirley," the letters give us the best descriptions of mining camp life ever written. Either Louise or Mary must have shown the letters to some of their friends; Bret Harte fashioned several of his stories after them.

Louise's observations were remarkably accurate, yet she never lost her femininity in describing the roughness of the miners and their lives. She also balanced her observations about what she saw with her own feelings about the events.

Only one other woman lived in the Rich Bar camp; the prostitutes had been run out just before Louise arrived. The other woman fainted at the sight of blood. Yet Louise could describe the hanging of a thief, just two weeks before Christmas in 1851:

"He had exhibited during the trial the utmost recklessness and nonchalance, had drank many times in the course of the day, and when the rope was placed around his neck, was evidently much intoxicated. All at once, however, he seemed startled into consciousness of the awful reality of his position, and requested a few moments for prayer.

"The execution was conducted by the jury, and was performed by throwing the cord, one end of which was attached to the neck of the prisoner, across the limb of a tree standing outside of the Rich Bar grave yard. Then all who felt disposed in so revolting a task lifted the poor wretch from the ground in the most awkward manner possible.

"The whole affair, indeed, was a piece of cruel butchery, though that was not intentional, but arose from the ignorance of those who made the preparations. In truth, life was only crushed out of him by hauling the writhing body up and down several times in succession wth the rope, which was wound around a large bough of his green-leafed gallows.

"Almost everybody was surprised at the severity of the sentence; and many, with their hands on the cord, did not believe even then that it would be carried into effect, but thought that at the last moment the jury would release the prisoner and substitute a milder punishment.

"The body of the criminal was allowed to hang for some hours after the execution. It had commenced storming in the earlier part of the evening; and when those whose business it was to inter the remains arrived at the spot, they found them enwrapped in a soft, white shroud of feathery snow flakes, as if pitying Nature had tried to hide from the offended face of heaven the cruel deed which her mountain children had committed."

The sun only reached the mining camp two hours each day. After a prolonged period of inactivity caused by a flood, the whole camp went on a long drunk. Louise considered drink and gambling the twin curses of mining life. Yet she sympathized with the men in describing their debauchery, which ended only when the last miner was down.

"Dame Shirley's" descriptions of mining camp characters rivalled Dickens in their vitality:

"Last night I had the honor of an introduction to His Honor. Imagine a middle-sized man, quite stout, with a head disproportionately large, crowned with one of those immense foreheads decked out with a slight baldness which enchant phrenologists, but which one never sees brooding above the soulful orbs of the great ones of the earth; a smooth fat face, grey eyes and prominent chin, the tout ensemble characterized by an expression of the utmost meekness."

The next July she wrote: "In the short space of twenty-four days, we have had murders, fearful accidents, bloody deaths, a mob, whippings, a

14

hanging, an attempt at suicide and a fatal duel."

She wrote of the attempted suicide's slashed throat and the hanged man's last writhings. She was horrified by the whippings unleashed on Spanish-speaking miners by the angry Anglos, yet she described them in detail:

"Oh, Mary! imagine my anguish when I heard the first blow fall upon those wretched men. I had never thought that I should be compelled to hear such fearful sounds, and, although I immediately buried my head in a shawl, nothing can efface from memory the disgust and horror of that moment. I had heard of such things, but heretofore had not realized that in the nineteenth century men could be beaten like dogs, much less that other men, not only could sentence such barbarism, but could actualy stand by and see their own manhood degraded in such disgraceful manner."

The Feather River camps played out later in 1852. Louise and Fayette returned to San Francisco. She never said much about him in her letters. Once in a while she mentioned having to perform her "wifely duties" as though she disliked them. Upon returning to San Francisco, they separated. Fayette went to the Sandwich Islands, and Louise got a divorce. She was satisfied that she had "seen the elephant."

Probably Louise's ability to observe and write accurately without being overwhelmed by the barbarity around her came from pride in herself as a person of strength. She did not have that in the east. She wrote:

"And only think of such a shrinking, timid, frail thing as I used to be a long time ago, not only living right in the midst of them , but almost compelled to hear if not see the whole."

After her divorce, Louise taught school in San Francisco, encouraging her best students to become writers. She returned East in 1878. She died at eighty-six, a resident in a home operated by Bret Harte's neices.

 Suggested reading: Louise Clappe, *The Shirley Letters from the California Mines* (New York: Alfred A. Knopf, 1949).

Legh Freeman

A BITTER NEWSPAPERMAN

Legh Freeman's enlistment in the Third Kentucky Confederate Cavalry seemed to set the theme for the rest of his life. Kentucky was a bitterly divided state. Nowhere did the numbers of men enlisting in opposing armies more equally balance.

The nineteen-year-old Virginian served as a telegrapher. He intercepted enemy telegrams to learn their plans and to send spurious Confederate telegrams to confuse.

Freeman was captured, imprisoned for thirteen months, and released on condition that he pledge loyalty to the Union and serve in its volunteer forces fighting Indians in the West. He took the oath but did not conceal his contempt for the Union whose uniform he then wore.

With his discharge from the Third United States Volunteers at Fort Kearney, Nebraska Territory, Freeman knew he could help his family by returning to Virginia. But he was unwilling to face enmity from friends and neighbors for having agreed to become a Galvanized Yankee.

By then fort telegrapher, Freeman decided to stay in the West. The next month, December, 1865, he became editor and publisher of the _Kearney Herald_.

When the Union Pacific's railroad came through Fort Kearney the next year, Freeman packed his new Washington Hand Press, his type, and his supplies into a wagon train and followed the track-building crews west.

During the next two years his celebrated "Press on Wheels" published newspapers in the Hell on Wheels track-laying towns from North Platte through Julesburg, Fort Sanders, Laramie City, and Green River City to Bear River City. The last place, more commonly called Beartown, was about thirteen miles east of present Evanston, Wyoming.

Freeman called Beartown the toughest track-end town of them all, the wickedest city in America. He supported the vigilantes in their efforts to clean up the railroad mob, mostly Irish workers employed by Cheesborough & Magee, a grading contractor.

Freeman pubished this notice in his paper: "The gang of garroters from the railroad towns east, who are congegating here, are ordered to vacate this city or hang withing sixty hours from this noon. By order of ALL GOOD CITIZENS."

But in November, 1868, after three of their men had been hanged, railroad workers tore down the jail which held more men awaiting summary execution, released the prisoners, and then headed for Freeman's newspaper plant. Alexander Toponce, who operated a slaughterhouse for the railroad crews, help Freeman escape by cutting a hole in his tent as the mob approached.

Toponce loaned Freeman a mule on which he rode twenty miles to Fort Bridger so fast you could have "played checkers on his coattails." When the rioting ended, fourteen men had been killed, thirty-five wounded, and Legh Freeman's printing plant destroyed.

Freeman moved to Ogden, Utah, where he started the *Ogden Freeman* newspaper. An admirer of the Mormons, he had promoted their president, Brigham Young, for the presidency of the United States in 1868.

Even though his support for Zion made Freeman an apologist for the Mountain Meadows Massacre, eventually he turned against the Mormons, attacking them as he had earlier attacked Chinese, Blacks, and Indians. He reported that Brigham Young, the "old scoundrel was upbraiding his daughter for being wild on the streets when the girl replied, 'Father, if Salt Lake City was fenced in and covered over it would be the biggest bawdy house in the world.'" Freeman considered himself the leader of a monogamous white race fighting against the polygamy of the various colored races.

Freeman married three times and was survived by four sons and a daughter. His will, leaving each son one dollar, recited that each had promised to follow the printing and publishing business if their father educated them, and their failure to do that forced him to mortgage his property to pay for their education. One boy had dropped out of school at ten; another ran away from home at fifteen.

Freeman's political loyalties shifted from democrat through populist to republican. In 1910, at age sixty-seven, he asked the legislature of the State of Washington to appoint him a United States Senator. Of the eight republican candidates in the preferential primary, he ran fifth, barely getting more than one percent of the vote. Four years later, he tried again, this time running for mayor of North Yakima; he got four percent of the votes cast. Eleven weeks later Freeman died.

Legh Freeman was a legendary newspaperman in the Old West, but he lived and died a bitter man.

Suggested reading: Thomas H. Heuterman, *Movable Type,* (Ames: The Iowa State Univ. Press, 1979).

LEGH FREEMAN AND SONS

American Heritage Center, Univ. Of Wyoming

KEEPING THE WHEELS ROLLING

The horses strained against their harnesses, slowly pulling the stage up to Pacheco Pass, southeast of San Francisco. Passenger Waterman Ormsby of New York was tired. He said he'd take a nap before supper.

"You should stay awake until we cross the pass," Tote Kenyon, fellow passenger and agent for the Butterfield Stage Lines, said. "Course I reckon you've seen the elephant by now."

A reporter for the *New York Herald,* Ormsby was a through passenger on the first westward crossing of the overland mail from Saint Louis to San Francisco. His reports, sent back as they met eastbound stages were devoured by eastern readers.

Exactly twenty-three days before, on September 16, 1858, Ormsby had boarded the stage at Tipton, Missouri, the end of the railroad. The first driver was John Butterfield, Junior. His father, a partner in the venture and an old stage driver, himself, was also aboard. Ormsby could not recall all the drivers and agents and passengers, but he was the only person to ride through from one end to the other.

Riding day and night for over three weeks had tired Ormsby's memory as well as his body. He did remember a Mexican woman with an eight-month old baby. That day's report contained a note of pathos, as Ormsby remembered his own son, nine months old when he left New York.

Ormsby carried a pistol, but only once was he afraid. That was in Apache country. As they approached the station at Stein's Peak, they knew that two hundred fifty of Mangas Coloradas's warriors had been there a few days before, demanding corn. Ormsby was relieved to see the post corral in the dim moonlight, rather that a heap of smoking ruins.

Ormsby contrasted the stations in Apache country, each with a single tent and corral, with some of those in Texas, placed beside forts holding two companies of cavalry. He suggested the government should station the troops where the trouble was.

Most stations were twelve to fifteen miles apart. Once in Texas they traveled one hundred thirteen miles without fresh animals. For that travel, along the Pecos River, they herded their replacement mules along with them. Ormsby commented on the many skeletons he saw, both of cattle and of persons, along that Texas road.

Different kinds of wagons were used. The most common one had three seats and was suspended on leather throughbraces. It had a boot in the rear for luggage.

They used mules in Texas, New Mexico, and Arizona, and horses in Missouri, Arkansas, Indian Territory, and California. Ormsby was unable to sleep in the crowded wagon the first two nights. His first bath was in the Clear Fork of the Brazos River in Texas. He got to bathe again in the Gila River of Arizona. Now he looked forward to a warm bath in San Francisco.

When John Butterfield left the stage at Fort Smith, he had given Ormsby a basket of cold cuts with the "needful to wash it down." Ormsby remembered it as his last civilized meal. His readers read about his morning meal at Connolly's Station in Texas. Breakfast there was coffee and shortcake, baked on coals. The two bachelors who kept the station had cups for coffee, but no plates or utensils. They passed the shortcake around, and each diner broke off a chunk and spread the butter with his pocket knife. The butter was a rare luxury.

When the stage finally reached the top of Pacheco Pass, the driver invited Ormsby up to the box. "Guess you've seen a mite of country, young feller."

Ormsby was glad he had stayed awake for the spectacular view, as the stage descended into Gilroy

"More than I knew there was," he replied.

"Well the next part yuh see will be goin' by durn fast. Hang onto yer hat."

The stage reached speeds of twenty miles an hour, and the driver laughed at the slower teamsters on the road. A moment of carelessness, a loose nut, or a broken strap would have sent them all to Kingdom Come.

When Ormsby protested, the driver yelled, "It's best to keep the wheels rolling or they'll slide."

They had supper in Gilroy and reached San Francisco the next forenoon. It had been quite a ride — twenty-eight hundred miles — and Ormsby had truly seen the elephant!

Suggested reading: Waterman L. Ormsby, *The Butterfield Overland Mail* (San Marino: Huntington Library, 1991).

CLASSIC ACCOUNT OF A LONG FIGHT

Con Orem, 29-year-old saloon keeper in Virginia City, Montana, claimed to be the middleweight champion of the world. He had had nine professional fights, mostly in the east. Saloon business was slow, and Orem read a notice placed in the *Montana Post* by Hugh O'Neil, challenging anyone to fight. Orem accepted and the fight was set for January 2, 1865, in Virginia City.

O'Neil, thirty-four, had only fought once professionally in California, but he had a good reputation as a bare-knuckle fighter in the mines. At one hundred ninety, he outweighed Orem by fifty-two pounds. O'Neil was the heavy betting favorite.

J. A. Nelson, selected as referee, built a special log arena for the fight behind his liquor store. The twenty-five hundred spectators constituted one-sixth of the territorial population. It would be like six million Californians coming to a fight today in San Francisco.

The London Prize Ring Rules governed. A round would end when a fighter was knocked or thrown down and could not get up immediately or when a fighter deliberately fell to end the round. One could take such a deliberate fall at any time, but his opponent could then jump on top of him, usually after a short run for increased impact. Wrestling was permitted, but hitting a man while he was down was not. After a man went down, his second dragged him to his corner. He was then allowed thirty seconds to rest, but if he could not get back to the scratch line in the center of the ring within eight seconds, he lost the fight.

The fighters wore thin, buckskin gloves, stretched tightly over hands that had been soaked in chemicals for hardening. This was the first glove fight in the territory. No limit was set on the number of rounds or the total elapsed time.

The Orem-O'Neil fight was the longest in the West. Thomas J. Dimsdale, Oxford-educated Englishman who edited the *Montana Post,* wrote the round-by-round account, a classic in frontier journalism.

The fight started at 1:34 p.m. According to Dimsdale, Orem was knocked down eleven times and wrestled down once; O'Neil was knocked down three times and wrestled down once. Orem deliberately slipped down ninety-one times to end a round, and O'Neil did it seven times. O'Neil fell on Orem twenty-four times; Orem on O'Neil seven times. Orem was on the ground 122 times, O'Neil forty-six times.

Here are some of Dimsdale's descriptions:

Round 17 – Heavy mauling from the word "time"; Con popped in his right on Hugh's olfactory department, which brought the ruby in a shower.

Round 30 - Con laughed and dropped a remembrance on Hugh's kissing trap with his right, but met a heavy lunge from Hugh's right on the knowledge box, and again on the ribs. Con slipped down and Hugh fell on him.

Round 37 - Con lost the fall, Hugh coming down heavily on him. Hugh took a pull at the bottle with renovating effect.

Round 54 - Con's left eye and cheek swelling.

Round 58 - Orem let drive with the heaviest lick of his right yet given. It sounded all over the building above the noise of the crowd.

Round 60 - Orem, though so much overmatched and overweighted, full of pluck and spirit, dropped in one on the cheek and retired to mother earth for the finish.

Round 65 - Con got in two right-handers, first on the optic and next on the choptic; Hugh closed and Con fell in a devout attitude.

Round 143 - Orem down; both much exhausted.

Round 155 - Both clinched; Hugh holding up Orem and pounding him on the head while on one knee, till he slipped down.

After round 185, the seconds and backers of the fighters — but not the fighters themselves — got the referee to call it a draw. All bets were off, and the $850 ring money was divided evenly. The fight had lasted three hours and five minutes.

During the fight a physician bled the inside of one of O'Neil's eyes and then closed it to keep O'Neil from going blind. While he was walking home after the fight, O'Neil did become temporarily blind. Two men pulled him on home in a wagon.

Orem wanted to walk home, but friends insisted on carrying him.

Orem and O'Neil fought each other again in Helena on August 24, 1866. This time O'Neil outweighed Orem by forty-seven pounds. The fight ended in the 51st round with an Orem victory, when O'Neil struck Orem while he was down.

Within a month Dimsdale, Montana's first newspaper editor, died from tuberculosis. Among his possessions was a ring given to him by his friend, Con Orem. He had also reported Orem's and O'Neil's second fight.

Dimsdale, an apologist for the Montana vigilantes, wrote *The Vigilantes of Montana,* still one of the leading books on that period of history. His description of a prize fight was as interesting as his book.

Suggested reading: Warren J. Brier, *The Frightful Punishment* (Missoula: Univ. of Montana Press, 1969).

A SHORT, SPECTACULAR CAREER

Albert D. Richardson cherished books from his early childhood. The Massachusetts native loved to read Emerson, and he taught school for a time. But a desire for a more active life drew him west.

After working as a news reporter in Cincinnati, he moved on to Kansas in 1857, when he was twenty-four.

Richardson fought with John Brown in the border wars of Kansas and Missouri, displaying courage and leadership ability. At twenty-five he was a leader of the Free-State men, and probably would have become prominent in Kansas politics had he not drifted on west to become one of the first settlers of Denver.

In May, 1859, Richardson met Horace Greeley when Greeley boarded the stage Richardson was riding to Denver. Greeley went on to the west coast, and Richardson turned south to El Paso. Returning by way of Santa Fe, he interviewed and rode with Kit Carson.

As war clouds grew darker, Richardson took a reporter's job on Greeley's *New York Tribune*. Then he joined the Union Army, becoming principal correspondent in Grant's army. After service in some early battles, he was captured on May 3, 1863, during Grant's Vicksburg campaign.

Richardson escaped from the Salisbury Prison on December 18, 1864. When he learned that his wife had died while he was in prison, leaving him with three small children, he moved back to the west. The children apparently remained with relatives.

Schuyler Colfax, Speaker of the House of Representatives, was planning a stage journey from Atchison, Kansas, to San Francisco. He had already invited William Bross, Lieutenant Governor of Illinois and correspondent for the *Chicago Tribune* and Samuel Bowles, correspondent for the *Springfield* (Mass.) *Republican* to go with him. Learning that Richardson was available and knowing of his reputation as a war correspondent, Colfax added him to the group. They left Atchison on May 22, 1865, reaching San Francisco on July 1.

Bowles wrote *Across the Continent,* a well-known book, to describe the trip. Richardson wrote his own widely-read book, *Beyond the Mississippi* about the same experiences. One excerpt from a side trip to Montana Territory on his return gives a flavor of Richardson's powers of observation and expression, and shows how he earned his reputation as a fine writer of the Old West.

While attending a dance at Virginia City, Richardson heard the leader of the three-man orchestra shout:

"Take your ladies for the next dance!

"Half a dozen swarthy fellows, fresh from the diggings, selected partners from the tawdry, bedizened women who stood in waiting. After each dance the miners led their partners to the bar for whisky or champagne; then, after a short pause, another dance; and so the sorry revelry continued from nine o'clock until nearly daylight, interrupted only by two fights. For every dance each masculine participant paid one dollar, half going to his partner, and half to the proprietor. The latter functionary, who was dealing monte with revolver at his belt, assured me that his daily profits averaged one hundred dollars. Publicly, decorum was preserved; and to many miners who had not seen a feminine face for six months, these poor women represented vaguely something of the tenderness and sacredness of their sex."

Richardson returned to New York and bought an interest in the *Tribune*, where he was offered a position as managing editor. He declined for health reasons and wrote a biography of General Grant.

Life probably seemed very good to Richardson in 1868. That year his friend from the long stagecoach ride to San Francisco, Schuyler Colfax, was elected vice president. He served with President Grant, the man Richardson had served with, admired, and about whom had written the biography.

In addition, Richardson fell in love. But his chosen was already married to Daniel McFarland, an Assistant Assessor for the City of New York. Mrs. McFarland got a divorce in Indiana, something the *Tribune's* competitor, the *New York Times*, called an outrage.

Matters came to a head on November 25, 1869, when McFarland hunted Richardson down in the counting room at the *Tribune* and shot him in the abdomen. McFarland's friends claimed he was so humiliated by the divorce and his wife's announcement of her engagement to Richardson that he should be excused for his crime of passion.

Richardson lived long enough for Henry Ward Beecher, America's most famous clergyman at the time, to perform the ceremony that joined him and his love in marriage. Vice President Colfax tried to visit his friend in the hospital, but came too late.

Richardson died on December 2, age thirty-seven. McFarland was prosecuted for murder the next spring and acquitted.

Suggested reading: Albert D. Richardson, *Beyond the Mississippi* (Hartford, 1890).

James Meline

24

WRITER ON HORSEBACK

James Meline was educated as a lawyer. After service as a U. S. Consul in Europe, he returned home to become a journalist. A New York native, he was the son of a French-born officer in the United States Army. James, too, joined the army. By Civil War's end, he was a colonel.

Colonel Meline wanted to write a book. He took a long horseback ride in 1866 to gather the material. His book is a fine account of life on the post-Civil War frontier.

Colonel Meline rode out of Fort Leavenworth, Kansas, on June 2. He rode northwest, up the valley of the Little Blue River. He was impressed with the fertile Kansas soil:

"Black as your hat," he wrote. "So rich that the earth looks as though it would laugh if you tickled it." He compared the rolling plains to the sea in language similar to that used earlier by William Cullen Bryant in his poem, *The Prairies.* Meline mentioned the "boundless sweep to the eye, with rolling waves of green from horizon to horizon – the same undulating play of sunshine and shade on its face – the same solitude – the same solemn and silent grandeur."

When he left Fort Leavenworth, Colonel Meline traveled for a time with a wagon train. Its guide was six feet tall, a daring rider and dead shot, who wore long hair and buckskin, and carried two pistols. The guide called himself Wild Bill. He claimed he had been a pony express rider as a boy and a scout and Civil War spy as a man. Perhaps Meline saw the confusion between Buffalo Bill Cody, who had been a pony express rider and scout, and Wild Bill Hickok, who had been a Civil War spy and scout. Meline wrote: "We do not feel obligated to believe all the stories."

Meline left the wagon train near Fort Sedgwick and headed southwest to Denver. He compared his first view of Long's Peak from a 135-mile distance to the first view of the Alps from a sixty-mile distance. The view of the American mountains was "incomparably finer, and I solemnly abandon the last of my European illusions on the subject of European scenery."

When he reached New Mexico, Meline made it clear that he admired the plains and mountains more than he did the native women. He recalled the three-page account in Kendall's *Santa Fe Expedition* of the "peerless beauty" on the adobe wall in Albuquerque, one hand supporting a pumpkin on her head and the other gracefully resting on her hip. With a tear of pity, she had given the pumpkin to a passing prisoner.

Twenty-five years later, Meline saw Albuquerque women on a more pleasant and attractive occasion. But he wrote: "If that young lady of the pumpkin, bare feet, taper fingers, hip, and all that sort of thing, left daughters resembling herself, I certainly did not see them."

As he approached Santa Fe Meline met an aged sheepherder named Candelaria, who had once found a nugget of gold worth $750. They visited a while, and the old man told the colonel how his name had grown like a gourd. From Candelaria it became Don Juan, Don Juan Candelaria, Señor Don Juan Candelaria, and Señor Don Juan Candelaria Caballero. But the gold lasted only twenty days. When it was gone, his name went back to Old Candelaria, and he returned to herding sheep.

Colonel Meline spent nine days in Santa Fe. The highlight of his visit there was meeting and talking to Kit Carson. The highlight of his book is his description of Santa Fe. He listed the archival documents available for historical study, and he provided his own thumbnail history.

His description of the city and its surroundings is remarkable in detail. He described the people, including the Indians, Mexicans, and Mountain Men. He described the markets, manufactures, agricultural production, mining, and tools. He described the customs and manners of the people, their educational systems, entertainments, and churches.

Some evidence of his detail is shown in his reporting of the animals stolen in 1863. In that year the Indians stole 24,389 sheep, 21 horses, 205 mules, and 402 cattle. The army took from the Indians 24,266 sheep, 152 horses, 232 mules, and 215 cattle. The Indians were ahead in cattle and sheep, the army in horses and mules.

Colonel Meline was fifty-four when he made his long ride. He averaged thirty-three miles on the days he rode. He developed his notes and sketched out the chapters of his book in the evenings and on the days he did not travel. He left for the states on August 11, returning to Fort Leavenworth by the Santa Fe Trail. He gave us a remarkable book on the Old West.

Suggested reading: James F. Meline, *Two Thousand Miles on Horseback: Santa Fe and Back* (Albuquerque: Horn & Wallace, 1966).

ABANDONED BOY

John Rowlands, born in Wales in 1841, was abandoned by his unwed mother and raised in a workhouse. He was the first of her four children, all from different fathers. The superintendent of the workhouse was a brutal man who beat the boys, took sexual liberties with the girls, and eventually died insane.

When he was fifteen, young John Rowlands thrashed the superintendent and ran away. He shipped out on a British ship and deserted at New Orleans. There he was adopted by a wealthy merchant, Henry Hope Stanley. The merchant gave the boy his name and called him Henry Morton Stanley.

Stanley enlisted in the Confederate Army when he was twenty. He was wounded and captured at Shiloh and then released from military prison to enlist in the Union Army. He got a medical discharge from that army when its authorities learned that he had not yet recovered from his wound. At that point young Stanley joined the Union Navy. He was probably the only man in the world to serve in three different military forces on both sides of the Civil War!

Stanley got interested in writing while he was in the Navy. When the Civil War ended, he traveled with Custer's 7th Cavalry as a reporter for the *Missouri Democrat* and a contributor to the *New York Herald* and other eastern newspapers.

Stanley covered the 1867 campaign against Indians in Kansas, mixing journalistic moralizing with vivid accounts of life in the frontier army as it chased Indians over the plains. In describing Wild Bill Hickok, a scout and tracker on the expedition, Stanley wrote:

"He has none of the swaggering gait, or the barbaric jargon ascribed to the pioneer. On the contrary, his language is as good as many a one that boasts college larnin'."

Early in the campaign, Stanley referred to the Indians' "bloody instincts, their savage hatred of the white race." By the end of the summer his racial attitude had moderated. Then he began to question frontier beliefs that the Indians always opposed the spread of civilization. He said the Indian would accept civilization if it was offered to

him: "Make him one of ourselves, bound by the same desires, possessing the same rights, and he will in time forget the savage pleasures of the past.

We know that if the red man could have been enslaved, he would have been before this; but there was a free spirit in his nature which made it impossible. The evidence shows plainly that the Indian has ever been the wronged, and that he fights because he believes that the white man was sworn to extirpitate (sic) him."

In October, 1867, Stanley went to southern Kansas to cover the meeting between Indians, the army, and government officials that resulted in the Medicine Lodge Treaty. He bragged about his warm welcome from Kiowa Chief Satanta, an Indian who Wild Bill Hickok said had killed more white men than any other on the plains. Stanley was impressed with Satanta's reply to the promises of the whites that they would build Indians comfortable houses, churches, and schools on the richest agricultural lands if they would only stop marauding.

Satanta had replied, "I love the land and the buffalo. I don't want any of these medicine homes (schools) built in the country; I want the papooses brought up exactly as I am. I love to roam over the wild prairie, and when I do it I feel free and happy, but when we settle down we grow pale and die."

Stanley's short career in the Indian Wars ended with the completion of the Medicine Lodge Treaty. He returned to England to report British campaigns in Africa. He would eventually be the founder of an African nation, would be elected to Parliament, and would be knighted.

Stanley used the same dramatic style in reporting news even when he, himself, made the news. In November, 1871, he stood on the shore of Lake Tanganyika, having just found the man he had been seeking for almost a year. Stanley reported his own words, "Doctor Livingstone, I presume."

Suggested reading: Henry M. Stanley, *My Early Travels and Adventures in America* (Lincoln: Univ. of Nebraska, 1982).

OREGON STYLE JOURNALISM

Citizens of the Old West wanted entertainment from their newspapers. Readers expected the same excitement they had heard about from distant cow or mining camps and could see first-hand in their own saloons. The editors, rough-talking, tough-fighting, often hard-drinking men, probably felt the violence of the times even more keenly than the men in the streets and were glad to oblige.

Politics, a common battleground, was always black or white, never gray. With libel laws in their infancy, journalism became highly personal, and rival papers swung free in editorial combat. The sharp-tongued, warlike brand of writing was best developed in Oregon, and the most vitriolic examples of such editorial invective in the West were labeled the Oregon Style.

In May 1867 brothers Henry and Thomas Gale established Roseburg Oregon's first newspaper, the *Ensign*. They had previously worked at the *Oregon State Journal* in Eugene City. In 1868, after their newspaper was well established, the Gales returned to Eugene City, leaving an editor named Webster in charge of the *Ensign*. The paper was a Republican organ, worshiping both Lincoln and President Grant.

In March 1870, William Thompson started the *Plaindealer* in Roseburg. Like the Gales, Thompson had come from Eugene City, where he had worked on a rival newspaper to the *Oregon State Journal* and then owned and edited another paper, the *Eugene Guard*. With the $1200 he got from selling the *Guard* and another $1000 raised by loyal democrats, Thompson was able to set up the *Plaindealer*.

Editor Webster was not as combative as the *Ensign*'s owners, and the first three months of competition was fairly tame. But when the Gales realized they were losing ground to the *Plaindealer*, they returned to Roseburg and took over the editorial direction of their paper. They wrote that Thompson's paper had "no wit, no sense, nothing but impotent malice."

Thompson responded to the "feeble lies about dead issues" with a pledge to "report the truth of issues muddied up by the green hands running the *Ensign*."

Journalism went downhill fast as comments were bandied back and forth about "lack of sense to comprehend the truth," "our bigoted neighbor, the overgrown urchin," "driving into the cesspool of ignorance while displaying the brains of boot leather," and "bare faced falsehoods by scaly alligators."

The December 3, 1870, issue of the *Ensign* filled nearly a page with degrading comments about the *Plaindealer*'s editor, calling him a "whey-faced falsifier with a whine somewhere between the bray of a donkey and a sick ape." It added, "A drunk man will get sober, but a fool will remain to the end of time, and so old whey-face is doomed."

Surprisingly, these weren't grouchy old men spouting anger from a lifetime of frustration. Thompson and Thomas Gale were twenty-two, Henry Gale a few years older.

The editorial diatribes erupted into bloodshed on Jackson Street on Sunday, June 11, 1871. Thompson, walking back from the post office, met the Gales leaving a saloon. Thomas Gale, a small man, complained about Thompson's last written attack.

"Well, what of it?" Thompson sneered.

Henry Gale, a much larger man, said Thompson should be ashamed of picking on his small brother. After exchanging a few more epithets, Henry Gale hit Thompson with his cane. Thompson punched back, and Thomas Gale, protecting his brother, drew his pistol and shot Thompson in the side.

Thompson drew his derringer and shot Thomas Gale in the side. Then he turned on Henry Gale and beat him over the head with his weapon.

Thomas Gale, wounded now, started beating Thompson on the head with his pistol. When Thompson turned to ward off this new attack, Henry Gale drew his pistol, shooting Thompson in the head. The bullet entered just to the rear and above the left ear. As Thompson turned back to his most recent assailant, he got another bullet in the left shoulder.

Somehow Thompson got off a shot at Henry, hitting him in the neck. Henry responded by pressing his pistol into Thompson's neck and firing a bullet that entered at the angle of the jaw and stopped in the mouth. Thompson tried unsuccessfully to speak and then collapsed to the ground.

We don't know if Thompson's inability to speak came from his shattered jaw, the bullet in his mouth, or the head wound in what is the verbal center in ninety percent of humans. We can also wonder at how much powder got loaded into pistol cartridges in those days. But the greatest wonder of all must be reserved for the fact that all three journalists survived.

Both newspapers also survived, although the journalistic bombast became somewhat muted for a time.

Suggested reading: Gary Meier, "Oregon's Gunfighting Editors," in *True West*, January, 1989.

NEWSPAPERMEN WHO ALWAYS MAKE MISCHIEF

As George Custer prepared to lead the 7th Cavalry out of Fort Lincoln in 1876, his superior, General Alfred Terry, received this telegram from General Sherman:

"Advise Custer to be prudent and not to take along any newspapermen, who always make mischief."

Originally Clement Lounsberry, owner of the *Bismarck Tribune*, planned to go with Terry's expedition. His plans changed, and he sent Mark Kellogg instead. Kellogg, a forty-seven-year-old widower with two daughters in Wisconsin, was assistant editor of Lounsberry's newspaper when it started in 1873. Before that he had been a telegrapher in Wisconsin.

Kellogg had lost his job with the *Tribune* and worked for a time in a haymaker's camp north of Bismarck. He rejoined the *Tribune* in 1876, in time to ride out with the 7th Cavalry. Lounsberry let Kellogg take his horse, and he gave him his Civil War belt to wear. He showed Kellogg the dried blood that could still be seen on the belt from Lounsberry's Civil War wound.

A storm delayed the march two days. Kellogg used the time to talk with Terry and his officers about their plans in leading twelve hundred men in a summer campaign. The Terry column would join other forces to drive the Indians back to the reservations where they belonged. Kellogg wrote:

"I have visited every department and every position of the camp, and find everywhere perfect preparation, order, and system. Everything is moving along like clockwork."

The column marched west for three weeks, and Kellogg sent back dispatches to the *Tribune* the *Chicago Times* and the *New York Herald*. He had little to write about at first, except the tedium of a military march on the plains. He described the creaking saddles, the braying mules, the squeaking axles, and the bellowing teamsters. He described Terry, a scholarly, Yale-trained lawyer, as a "gentleman soldier," a "popular, kind, and considerate commander." He was also accurate in his description of Custer. The fearless, dashing officer of "unbounded energy" and "electric mental capacity" had an "iron constitution." He was always out in front, "hell-whooping" over the plains."

Kellogg's stories were carried back by army couriers with their military dispatches. One story was almost lost. It was to be carried by three soldiers, going back by steamboat. Their rowboat sank going out to the steamboat, and a sergeant drowned. The mail sack was fished out of the river, and Kellogg spent the night drying his pages.

Kellogg traveled as a guest of the 7th Cavalry. Lounsberry and Custer had known each other back in Michigan. Custer's two brothers,

Tom, a captain, and Boston, a civilian employee, rode with the 7th, as did their nephew, Autie Reed, going along for the fun. Kellogg felt himself a part of the Custer campaign family.

Kellogg's last dispatch was a two-thousand word story he sent to the *Herald*. He worked until after midnight on June 21 to finish it. He mentioned that officers had asked their friends to watch the *Herald*, knowing that Kellogg would record their deeds there. He also wrote a short note to Lounsberry, saying, "We leave the Rosebud tomorrow, and by the time this reaches you we will have met and fought the red devils, with what results remains to be seen. I go with Custer and will be at the death."

Three days later Custer divided his regiment into four parts. Kellogg rode with the five companies personally led by Custer. They were all killed.

Custer's defeat was one of the great news stories of the nineteenth century. The story reached the east on July 6, in the middle of the nation's celebration of its one hundredth birthday. Telegrapher J. M. Carnahan in Bismarck "jerked lightning" for all but three hours in a forty-eight hour period to send the forty thousand words of press dispatches. But not one word could come from the only reporter who had been on the scene.

William Cullen Bryant, editor of the *New York Evening Post*, wrote Kellogg's elegy in prose, published on July 11. He said:

"If it is heroic to face danger and meet death calmly in the discharge of duty, then Mark Kellogg, the correspondent of the *New York Herald* who died with Custer, was a hero. His duty as a correspondent was to go with Custer, and he went in pursuit of duty, not of honors. The danger was as great to him as to any soldier in the column that he marched with, and he encountered it as cooly as they."

Suggested reading: John C. Hixon, "Custer's Mysterious Mr. Kellogg," in *North Dakota History, v.* 17 (3) (July, 1950).

Richard B. Hughes

NOT A TIME TO KILL

Richard B. Hughes and M. D. Rochford grew up together in Nebraska. In April, 1876, when both were twenty, they went to the Black Hills to prospect for gold. They found nothing. Hughes, who had worked on a newspaper before, got a job reporting for the *Deadwood Pioneer*.

He had much to report. Although the government had set aside the Black Hills as an Indian reservation, thousands of prospectors had invaded from every direction. All of them were breaking the law, but no one enforced the law.

Miner's courts, acting without legal authority, were created after killings. The customary verdict was not guilty.

Four men were buried in Deadwood in one day. Besides claim jumping among prospectors, other problems arose from gamblers and confidence men moving in, seeking new blood.

Overriding all these concerns were the Indians. The recent victory over Custer at the Little Bighorn gave the reservation Indians new courage to fight back. Both settlers and prospectors lived in great fear.

While many reporters gained fame in reporting violence, Richard Hughes' power of expression received its greatest challenge in preventing a murder, not in reporting one. In 1877, he and Rochford started out for another try at the gold fields. They left Deadwood in February with two pack mules.

When they stopped for lunch one day, they saw the finest pack outfit they had ever seen. Big Louis Meyer, six feet, three inches tall and perfectly proportioned, rode a beautiful chestnut mare, leading two white pack mules. When Meyer saw the two young partners preparing their meal, he called out, "Hello, boys, don't you want one more for dinner?"

Meyer invited Hughes and Rochford to share his cabin, only a mile from where they planned to prospect. "I'd be mighty glad if you'd come to camp with me," he said. "There's plenty of room, plenty of feed for the mules, and not another man within ten miles that I know of."

They accepted Meyer's invitation and moved in. A week later, another prospector moved into the area and camped about two miles from them. This new prospector, named Mac, had a poor reputation. He had once refused food to a hungry man, unable to pay.

Meyer did not like their new neighbor. When he found that the man also had a mean-looking, scrawny stallion which he allowed to run on the open range, Meyer was indignant. Afraid that his beautiful mare would be contaminated, he told Mac that if he didn't confine his stallion, he would come shooting, and he wouldn't care who he was shooting at.

About this time, Hughes and Rochford split up over an incident so minor that Hughes could not even remember what it was about when he wrote his book. Rochford went back to Deadwood, and Hughes stayed with Meyer. When it was time for Hughes to move to his own claim, Meyer was sad about his new friend's departure. Then Hughes learned that Meyer had blamed his split-up with Rochford on Mac. The night before he was to leave, Hughes was shocked to hear Meyer say, "Dick, I'm going to kill old Mac tomorrow."

"You're going to what?" asked an astonished Hughes.

"I've got the place picked out where the trail crosses the creek. I'll just knock him off there and cave the bank over him so the devil himself will never find him."

Hughes was unable at first to find words. It was obvious the old prospector was serious. When Hughes was able to talk, he tried to reason logically with Meyer, but the man's mind was already working logically. He said Mac's reputation was bad and everyone knew he had refused food to a hungry man. Besides, he had violated the law of the open range, and now he had caused two young men who grew up together to part company.

The last point was the main one. Meyer said that between him and his first partner what was his was his partner's and what was his partner's was his. Meyer's heart had broken when the partner died. Then the old man's voice broke.

"Yes, he died on me," he sobbed. "His horse fell on him and broke his leg. God knows, I did everything I could for Fred, but I was young and didn't know how to fix him up right."

He peered into Hughes' face, tears streaming down his own. "Dick, don't you think that if any man ever made trouble between Fred and me, either one of us would have killed him, and it would serve him right?"

Hughes argued, but Meyer began to get mad. Meyer said he had been a fool to announce his intention in advance. He should have just killed Mac and said nothing. Not until Hughes thought of the argument that innocent children might suffer if Mac were killed, would Meyer listen. Finally, after more protestations by Hughes, Meyer promised to not kill the man.

A relieved Hughes took his leave the next morning. He featured the incident in his book about his newspaper career in the Black Hills. It had taken all his communication skills to prevent a murder.

Suggested reading: Richard B. Hughes, *Pioneer Years in the Black Hills* (Glendale: Arthur H. Clark Company, 1957).

WRITER FOR THE INDIANS

George Bird Grinnell made his first tour of the west in 1870, when he was a twenty-year-old senior at Yale. He was born in Brooklyn and raised near Audubon Park on Manhattan. Perhaps his middle name had something to do with his lifelong interest in ornithology, zoology, and natural history. He was, for a time, a student of Lucy Audubon, widow of the artist-naturalist. Later Grinnell founded the Audubon Society.

Grinnell encountered hostile Indians two times on his first trip to the West. The first was an Indian attempt to steal horses. Second, and much more serious, was an attack on Grinnell, Luther North, and a third man. The three men traded gunfire with the warriors — probably Sioux or Cheyenne — and drove them off.

Grinell became a hunter, explorer, mountain climber, and conservationist. More than any other person, he was responsible for the creation of Glacier National Park. But for his natural modesty, it would have been named for him. As it is, the park contains Grinnell Mountain, Grinnell Glacier, and Grinnell Lake.

In 1872 Grinnell returned to the west to hunt buffalo with the Pawnees. He studied their customs and wrote down their folk tales.

Two years after that, he traveled with George Custer's 7th Cavalry expedition to the Black Hills. By then Grinnell was on the staff of the Peabody Museum at Harvard and working on his Ph. D.

Grinnell was assigned to Custer's 1874 expedition to collect paleontological materials. On this expedition, he formed a close friendship with Custer's favorite scout, Lonesome Charley Reynolds.

In 1875 Grinnell made a reconnaissance of Yellowstone National Park. On that trip he began writing about the wanton destruction of buffalo, elk, and deer for their hides. Grinnell loved to hunt, but he was always a conservationist. In 1887 he would assist Theodore Roosevelt in forming the Boone and Crockett Club, an association of hunter-conservationists.

In 1876 Custer invited Grinnell to come west for another expedition with his 7th Cavalry. Grinnell asked permission from his supervising professor at Harvard, but was turned down. Had he gone, he might have been killed at the Little Bighorn, next to his friend, Charley Reynolds.

Instead of being killed by Indians, Grinnell became their faithful supporter during the next half-century. He began his writing career in 1876 as natural history editor of *Forest and Stream*. In 1880, when he

GEORGE BIRD GRINNELL

Library of Congress

completed his Ph.D., he became editor of the magazine, and he eventually owned it.

Grinnell's close friendship with Theodore Roosevelt started when he wrote a barbed review of Roosevelt's *Hunting Trips of a Ranchman* in 1885. When Roosevelt confronted Grinnell about his review, Grinnell persuaded him that all his comments were accurate. Besides each having a degree from Harvard, both men had inherited money and social position and both were interested in the environment and the West. They stayed friends for life

Grinnell also wrote many articles for other publications, both popular magazines and professional journals. He wrote over twenty volumes on Indians, hunting, and conservation, plus many books for juveniles, including the "Jack" series — *Jack Among the Indians; Jack, the Young Cowboy; Jack in the Rockies*, for example.

Grinnell first became interested in the Blackfeet in 1885. For many years, even continuing after his marriage in 1902, he camped with them every summer. He formed a close friendship with James Willard Schultz, a New Englander who went west to live with the Blackfeet and write many books, himself. Grinnell was adopted into the Blackfeet tribe and made an honorary chief.

Grinnell's most important books were about the Cheyennes. *The Fighting Cheyennes, The Cheyenne Indians* (two volumes), and *By Cheyenne Campfires* are the product of a lifetime of careful observation, detailed interviews, and thoughtful research. The Cheyennes were the best story-tellers in America. Perhaps Grinnell's interest in that tribe grew out of professional admiration and respect.

When President Coolidge presented a medal to Grinnell in 1925, the president said Glacier Park was Grinnell's monument. The world can be thankful that his work at Harvard kept Grinnell from going to the Little Bighorn.

Grinnell died in 1938 at the age of eighty-eight.

Suggested reading: George Bird Grinnell, *Pawnee, Blackfoot, and Cheyenne* (New York: Charles Scribner's Sons, 1961).

A REFORMER TRAVELS A LONELY ROAD

By the time he was sixteen, Thomas Henry Tibbles had fought with the Abolitionists in Kansas, where he was twice captured, sentenced to death, and escaped. At twenty-one he married, and he served as a newspaper correspondent in the Civil War.

After the war, he became a Methodist preacher while working for Omaha newspapers. He retired from the ministry in 1877, taking up the cause of the Ponca and Omaha Indians.

"I assault a system," Tibbles claimed. "If the angel Gabriel were president and he should select his cabinet from the courts of heaven, neither he nor his cabinet could prevent the wrongs against which I protest, so long as the present system is in force." Another time he said, "A reformer travels a lonely road."

In 1879 he reported the trial of Standing Bear vs. General George Crook, one of the most famous Civil Rights cases in U. S. history.

When Tibbles' wife died, he married Bright Eyes, daughter of the last head chief of the Omahas. He homesteaded in Nebraska, and then lectured widely for Indian rights.

Tibbles retired from farming in 1888 and rejoined the editorial staff of the *Omaha World-Herald*. In 1890 Tibbles and his wife witnessed the killing of Indians by the 7th Cavalry at Wounded Knee. He sent his dispatches back east, the first press releases to the public.

In 1903, Bright Eyes died. Tibbles continued as editor for the *World-Herald*. He married again in 1907. He died in Omaha in 1928, aged eighty-eight. He was still writing for the Omaha *World-Herald* until a few days before his death.

For Tibbles the road of the reformer was filled with enough adventures to last a dozen lifetimes. In looking back, the high point seemed to come after the trial of Standing Bear. The chief had taken Tibbles aside and told him if he ever had trouble, he knew where to come for help.

"You have a good house now to live in," the chief said. "A little while ago I had a house and land and stock. Now I have nothing. It may be that sometime you may have trouble. You might lose your house. If you ever want a home, come to me or my tribe. You shall never want as long as we have anything. While there is one Ponca alive, you will never be without a friend."

Thomas Henry Tibbles' road as a reformer may have been lonely. But from then on, he was never completely alone.

Suggested reading: Thomas Henry Tibbles, *Buckskin and Blanket Days* (Garden City: Doubleday, 1957).

WESTERN HOME

Physician Brewster Higley moved from Ohio to Smith County, Kansas, in 1871, when he was about sixty years old. He lived in a one-room dugout along Beaver Creek. He enjoyed the scenery, but not the winters.

Higley wrote a poem which he called "Western Home." In it he praised the scenery along Beaver Creek and in the Solomon River Valley, and he mentioned antelopes grazing on green hillsides below white bluffs.

In 1873 the *Smith County Pioneer*, a weekly newspaper, published the poem. Higley received so much praise from neighbors that he asked Dan Kelley, a carpenter who played with the Harlan Brothers Band, to set the poem to music. The band with their vocalist, Cal Harlan, who was Kelley's brother-in-law, played the song at dances, parties, and celebrations throughout Smith County.

The song spread slowly by memory and word of mouth throughout the West, but it was apparently not published until 1910 when it appeared in *Cowboy Songs and Other Frontier Ballads*, compiled by John A. Lomax.

Two years before, Lomax, a professor at the University of Texas and Sheldon Fellow for the Investigation of American Ballads at Harvard University, had gone to the Buckhorn Saloon in San Antonio, seeking old cowboy songs. The bartender told him of an old Black man who used to follow the Chisholm Trail as a cook and knew a few old songs.

Lomax found the man leaning against a mulberry tree at the rear of his place of business, "a low drinking dive." The old cook said, "I's too drunk to sing today. Come back tomorrow."

Lomax returned the next morning, took the man down to the Buckhorn, where he had set up his heavy Edison recording machine, and got many songs, incuding the words and tune for Dr. Higley's *Western Home.*

In spite of its publication in 1910, the song attracted little attention for almost twenty years. Then on the night that New York Governor Franklin Roosevelt was elected president, a group of newspaper reporters gathered on his doorstep to serenade him. Their songs included the one Dr. Higley had written, and Roosevelt asked to have it repeated, saying, "That's the best song I've ever heard." It soon was the favorite song in the White House, and through the enthusiasm of the president became an American favorite. Radio stations everywhere were playing it in the 1930s.

Here are the words, as originally published in Smith Center, Kansas, in 1873:

Oh, give me a home where the buffalo roam,
Where the deer and the antelope play,
Where never is heard a discouraging word
And the sky is not clouded all day.

Chorus:

A home, a home, where the deer and the antelope play,
Where never is heard a discouraging word
And the sky is not clouded all day.

Oh, give me the gale of the Solomon vale
Where life streams with buoyancy flow,
On the banks of the Beaver, where seldom if ever
Any poisonous herbage doth grow.

Oh, give me the land here the bright diamond sand
Throws light from the glittering stream,
Where glideth along the graceful white swan,
Like a maid in her heavenly dream.

I love the wild flowers in this bright land of ours,
I love, too, the curlew's wild scream,
The bluffs of white rocks and the antelope flocks
That graze on our hillsides so green.

How often at night, when the heavens are bright
By the light of the glittering stars,
Have I stood there amazed and asked as I gazed,
If their beauty exceeds this of ours.

The air is so pure, the breezes so light,
The zephyrs so balmy at night,
I would not exchange my home here to range
Forever in azure so bright.

In spite of the last verse, both Dr. Higley and Kelley found the Kansas winters too severe. Higley moved to Arkansas and Kelley to Iowa.
We no longer call Higley's song "Western Home," but it has long been an American favorite as *Home on the Range*.

Suggested reading: David Dary, *True Tales of Old-Time Kansas* (Lawrence: Univ. Press of Kansas, 1984).

GHOST WRITER

When Ash Upson showed up in Silver City, New Mexico Territory, in early 1874, no one would have thought the grizzled old reprobate with the dirty, slouch hat and tobacco-stained whiskers had come from a fine Connecticut family. In fact, Ash had been well educated in expensive eastern schools, and had even been a reporter on the *New York Herald*. But standing there in Catherine Antrim's boarding house, fishing coins out of the bundle tied on his back, he looked just like another saddle tramp down on his luck.

Upson couldn't help notice Catherine's fourteen-year-old son, Billy. Always in trouble, Billy was a notorious juvenile delinquent. Perhaps Ash was interested in the boy because he saw the same rebellious spirit there that had made him leave a pleasant eastern life for the rough frontier.

Catherine died of cancer that September, the day before Billy's fifteenth birthday. Billy's stepfather started drinking heavily, and, with no one to control him, Billy went completely wild.

During the next few years, Ash worked on various newspapers in Central City, Fort Stanton, Las Vegas, Elizabethtown, and Mesilla, and founded the *Albuquerque Press.* Sometimes he mixed in work as a stagecoach agent, and, for a time in 1876, he clerked at a store in Roswell, where he also served as postmaster and justice of the peace.

With jurisdiction over hundreds of square miles around Roswell, Justice of the Peace Upson settled disputes and performed marriages, always keeping a bottle of booze next to his "law" books. Once, a randy cowboy who thought he was deeply in love rushed in, demanding to be married at once. Ash complied, and the happy cowboy rode away with his true love.

A few days later the cowboy galloped back to town, stormed into Ash's office, and demanded a divorce.

"Calm down and have a snort," Ash said, pushing the bottle across his judicial bench.

"I don't need a drink. I need a divorce."

"No, lad, you don't need a divorce."

"Like hell I don't. You know what that chippie done?"

"I don't know and I don't care. You ain't even married, so you sure don't need a divorce."

The cowboy's jaw dropped in disbelief. "What the hell you mean?"

"You heard me right. I sized that gal up soon's you brought her in. I knew she wasn't ready for the bridal path."

"But you said the words."

"I never recorded it in the books. So you ain't married, son. Now have another drink and quit worrying."

"Well, I'll be damned," the relieved cowboy said.

Ash continued to hear of Billy Antrim from time to time, and knew the boy was still in trouble — sometimes, now, in killing trouble.

In 1880, Ash became special "clerical" deputy for Sheriff Pat Garrett, who had just been elected and could not read or write. Garrett needed someone to handle the bookwork in the office, and Ash took the job. From then on, he was Pat Garrett's closest friend.

Within a year, Billy had been killed by Garrett, and Ash became the ghost writer of the book that explained how it happened. The book also contained many details of Billy's youth, some of which seemed to come from Ash Upton's imagination, even though he had boarded for several months with Billy and his mother.

The Authentic Life of Billy the Kid, published in 1882, made Garrett famous. He and Ash stayed close, and Ash eventually moved into Garrett's home, became godfather to the Garrett children, and flustered Apolinaria Garrett with his untidy habits and salty language.

"Why you keep him in my house?" Apolinaria demanded.

"He's a great man," Pat always replied.

Pat seemed to think Ash Upson was some kind of a genius. But for bad luck, a business suggestion by Ash might have made them both rich.

Ash suggested that they acquire land in the Pecos River Valley and irrigate it with a series of dams. Pat and Ash got the project started, but they had to accept the help of a Colorado investor, who forced out the two founders and got rich himself.

A broke and embittered Pat Garrett moved to Uvalde, Texas, taking Ash Upson with him. Ash died in Pat Garrett's Uvalde home on October 6, 1894.

Ash Upson's name today is largely forgotten, but his ghost writing made Billy the Kid's name a household word.

Suggested reading: Sam Henderson, "Ash Upson — Pat Garrett's Sidekick and Ghost Writer," in *Golden West* (March, 1974).

THE ELEGANCE OF SOME EARLY WRITING

Dakota Territory made a poor impression on Thomas E. Cooper when he first saw it in 1864. Cooper crossed the northern part of the territory in a train of 123 ox-drawn wagons, seeking Rocky Mountain gold. He said he would not give "the shadow of a lamb's tail for all the Dakota dirt he passed over."

But fourteen years later, after disappointment in Montana prospecting and Minnesota farming, he homesteaded in the Park River Valley, northwest of Grand Forks.

By 1883 Cooper was already considered an old-timer. The *Grand Forks Herald* asked him to write a brief sketch of the early days in Walsh County. Like many persons of that era, Cooper was well read but had limited experience in writing. Brevity and conciseness would not be respected for another two or three generations. The result was a contrived fanciness that passed for elegance and erudition.

Cooper had decided to settle in North Dakota because of the enthusiastic description he heard from his pastor, Rev. R. R. Gowdy. In a well-crafted sentence, although three times as long as is now favored, Cooper wrote:

"Mr. Gowdy's words, coming as they did with so much candor, from a gentleman of unquestioned integrity and intellectual ability, did, I confess, so influence me that I resolved to see for myself if his opinions were based on such facts as to warrant pulling up anchor and leaving the old moorings where for twenty years I had enjoyed social relations with good neighbors and friends."

After crossing the "Raging Red River" to Grand Forks, Cooper went to the house of "mine host" for his first Dakota meal. In searching for available land to claim, "the Knight of the Quill" said he and three friends "looked at Uncle Sam's big pasture field to see if we could find a suitable harbor in which to cast anchor." They "sailed about on the prairie all day like a brig in a fog without rudder or chart." One wonders if the pun was intentional when he said they "partook of meals with good relish."

At night the four land-seekers bedded down in the twelve by fourteen "castle in the woods" owned by one McGregor, who sold merchandise while he farmed. Four "full-fledged sinners in one bed required the breathing power to be considerably exercised to perform their functions." But after a bear tried to enter the cabin, two men were placed on guard, giving the other two "sufficient space for repose."

Cooper liked the valley of the Park River, and he filed his homestead claim there in December, 1878. The settlers were depending on a Swede who lived eight miles west of Cooper's claim to bring mail from a stage station on the Red River, twelve miles east of Cooper. No good road had been built, the snow was deep, and the Swede, who had no horse, soon gave up.

Cooper then circulated petitions to establish three post offices closer to the settlers. He chose the names when he sent the petitions to Washington. He selected Park River for one and Sweden (near present Nash) for another. Expecting to be named postmaster for the third, Cooper and his family discussed several names. They chose Grafton, the name of the New Hampshire county where his wife's parents had been raised. He said it was easy for all to pronounce, and it reminded him of his fruit-raising, tree-grafting experiences in Minnesota, which he hoped to repeat in North Dakota.

In later years, his neighbors thought he should have selected Coopertown or Cooperton. Cooperstown, North Dakota, was named for another Thomas Cooper, no relation.

Cooper built the first hotel in Grafton and was one of the founders of the city.

Like many writers, when Cooper got wrapped up in his subject, his fanciness and pretense disappeared. He closed his brief memoir:

"When I consider the condition of Walsh County, even three years since, and contrast it with the present, I am lost in amazement at the rapid progress made in so short a space of time. Then there were scarcely garden patches under cultivation, now I know men who are farming six or seven hundred acres. Then the only Grafton was a log cabin. Now we have a city government with a population bordering on five thousand people.

"Had I not drawn this sketch out to so great a length, I might give some incidents in early pioneer life worth recounting, but I am admonished that I should draw to a close, so I will bid the *Herald* readers good night."

Suggested reading: T. E. Cooper, "Sketches of Early Settlements of Portions of Walsh County," in *Collections of the State Historical Society of North Dakota*, v. 2 (1908).

WRITING AS HARD AS NAILS

The transformation of the lonely cowboy — overworked, underpaid, lonesome, womanless, and usually unschooled — into the West's most exciting figure was largely the work of two men. Charlie Russell did it with drawings and paintings. Frederic Remington used both visual art and his writing pen. In fact, his accomplishment as an artist barely overshadowed his writing skill.

Theodore Roosevelt, himself a great western cattleman, said it best in an 1897 letter to his friend, Remington: "You come closer to the real thing with the pen than any other man in the western business. And I include Hough, Grinnell and Wister."

Wister, also Roosevelt's friend, would later call Remington "A national treasure." And Wister wrote The Virginian, usually called the first great western novel.

Remington, New York son of a newspaper publisher, dropped out of Yale in 1880. He had been a football star — teammate of the great Walter Camp — and was an outstanding boxer. He even considered a professional career in boxing. But he headed west to camp under Montana skies and sketch its cowboys. Then he bought a sheep ranch in Kansas, where he enjoyed the open land, coursing jackrabbits, and all-night saloon drinking with cowboys. However he made no money ranching.

Remington kept remembering the words of an old bullwhacker he had camped with back on the Yellowstone in Montana. "The railroad's comin'," the old timer had said. "Purty soon we'll have them damned derby hats, smoky chimbleys, and grain binders. This big country's on its way out, and won't nobody recollect it."

Remington resolved to prove the old man wrong. He headed southwest to sketch Cheyennes and Comanches in Indian Territory, hunt with vaqueros in Mexico, and ride with Apaches and cowboys in Arizona. After searching for a legendary lost mine in Arizona, he rode with the Army in its pursuit of Geronimo.

Then Remington's drawings began appearing in Harper's Weekly, each with a written account of the incident portrayed. As his artwork spread to Outing Magazine, Youth's Companion, and Century, the written accounts grew longer and began appearing over Remington's by-line.

The editors of Century were the first to recognize Remington's potential as a writer. They commissioned him to write Horses of the Plains, a subject on which he had become an expert. No one could draw horses better than Remington. And no one could write better about the men who rode them in the Old West. Century soon followed with A Scout with *the Buffalo Soldiers, On the Indian Reservations,* and *Artist Wandering Among the Cheyennes.*

Remington built a large home in New Rochelle, New York. A double door to his studio allowed the entry of horses he kept stabled on the grounds for models. But he continued his trips west, where he lived in soldiers' barracks and cow camps, listening to tales of the vanishing past. He became a close friend of General Nelson Miles and rode with him in Dakota and Montana as the Army tried to drive the Sioux to reservations. He also became close friends with many Plains Indians, whom he admired and respected.

Remington correctly predicted in summer 1890 that the Indians would make a final show of defiance the next winter. After producing material that year for forty-three issues of *Harper's Weekly* and five issues of *Harper's Monthly,* he went to the Dakotas in December to ride again with a scouting party. He was riding in the Bad Lands when news came of the showdown at Wounded Knee, far to the south. He hurried to the site of the battle to interview and sketch the survivors.

Fifteen of Remington's *Harper's* articles were published in his first book, *Pony Tracks.* All of his writing was documentary in character. It had a hard-as-nails quality of realism which the esthetic qualities were never allowed to overshadow. When he started writing fiction, he never compromised his principles, and that work seems just as real as the non fiction. It was one of his short stories, *Massai's Crooked Trail,* that prompted Roosevelt, who was Wister's friend as well, to write the compliment mentioned above.

Remington faced extraordinary competition as a writer of the Old West — Wister, Bret Harte, Alfred Henry Lewis, Joaquin Miller, and others. Such men concentrated their considerable talents on writing. Remington divided his among art work (some of which illustrated these others' writings), sculpture, and writing. That writing stands with the best.

No one except Bodmer recorded the West in art as well as Remington. No one except Russell drew with as much heart or enthusiasm. Remington never drew or wrote a false scene. His books authentically record the Old West.

Suggested reading: Harold McCracken, "Frederic Remington — Writer," in *The Westerners, N. Y. Posse Brand Book,* (New York: 1956).

THE FORT CUSTER NEWS

Soldier correspondents writing columns in civilian newspapers tell us much about Old West history. We are usually entertained by their carefree, often cynical, humor; we are sometimes surprised by their grasp of social and political issues; and we are often informed historically by their first-person accounts.

Private James O. Purvis, Company B, 1st Cavalry, is a good example. Purvis was stationed at Fort Custer, at the mouth of the Little Bighorn River in Montana. He wrote a column, the Fort Custer News, published at erratic intervals in the *Billings Daily Gazette.*

In April 1886 Purvis wrote about April showers bringing May flowers and the promise of bountiful crops in the company gardens. The companies were assigned gardening plots along the river, about two miles from the fort. One company raised a small barrel of whiskey to drink prosperity to the crops of '86. Purvis wrote:

"After a liberal irrigation in honor of their new 'spuds,' they drank success to agriculture generally throughout the territory. The sentiment was good enough, but the whiskey was of that quality which usually incites its patrons to become sluggers. The effect it had upon our agricultural friends proved no exception. One of the parties was badly hurt and the others not improved any."

In the same column Purvis mentioned that a sentry had been posted the winter before in the rear of the officers' quarters. This interfered with the "garrison dudes" who had been calling on the "kitchen belles along the line." That spring the sentry was removed, and the dudes were again happy in the performance of their "nightly back-gate osculatory exercises."

Purvis wrote about a dance held by the Maennerchor, a men's singing group. When Private Perkins of the band stepped out on the stage to make an announcement, someone cried out, "Down in front." Purvis said Perkins suddenly reached for his mustache, then smiled and continued with the announcement. Perkins was too sensitive, Purvis thought. No one would think his mustache was only "down." The girl in the back seat, who cried out, only wanted a better look at him.

In a June column Purvis described a picnic on the bank of the Little Bighorn. The picnickers arrived at 2:30, and the ladies came in two ambulances from the fort. In an "incredibly short space of time, preparations to extinguish thirst were in progress." Willing hands spread a bountiful repast, including a large tub of ice cream. They cleared away brush and stretched a tarpaulin on the ground for a dance floor. Dancing started at 3:30 and continued to midnight.

Purvis was a sensitive observer of social issues. He wrote about an order to shoot all dogs trespassing on the parade ground. He observed that Fort Custer was a reservation within a reservation. The difference between dogs and Indians was that dogs were run off the reservation and Indians were run on.

Like all early forts on the plains, Fort Custer was built by the first soldiers who occupied it. Most of the labor in improvement and maintenance was also provided by soldiers. Purvis addressed the pervasive problem of the army in dividing responsibilities between civilian tradesmen who expected competitive wages and soldiers who had enlisted to fight. He said work and drill, the main features of military life, were as antagonistic as fire and water. Both were essential in a frontier garrison, but no amount of finesse by the post administration could make a laborer and soldier out of the same person.

A person on fatigue duty all day "cuts a sorry figure at dress parade in the evening. He may have time to wash his face, but he is neither a credit to himself nor to his officers."

In June 1886 Purvis wrote about an historic event, the return of the survivors of the 7th Cavalry to the scene of the Little Bighorn Battle, which was fought ten years before. Sioux Chief Gall also came.

Captain Godfrey's account and Gall's account became classics in the abundant literature about the battle. Purvis reported both accounts first hand.

Suggested reading: Richard Upton, *Fort Custer on the Bighorn* (Glendale: Arthur Clark Company, 1973).

WRITING WHAT YOU KNOW

Patrick McGeeney was a babe in his mother's arms when his parents came from Ireland in the 1870s to settle in Newton, Kansas, the toughest town on the Chisholm Trail. They came a few years after the Newton General Massacre, the bloodiest three-minute gunfight in the Old West, and Patrick, growing up there, would have known of the history.

In 1893, the nineteen-year-old was a brakeman on the Santa Fe Railroad in Oklahoma. In May that year, Henry Starr, Bill Doolin, and Bitter Creek Newcomb rode into Ponca, Indian Territory, to rob Patrick's train when it stopped there. But the alerted train crew stopped at the cattle pens, short of the passenger station. Patrick, unarmed, walked forward to see what was up.

"If I send back any kind of signal, it's your cue to get the train out of danger," he told the conductor.

The three bandits, holding hostages, added Patrick to the group and ordered him to signal the train forward. Patrick's bravery foiled the robbery, and the bandits rode away, empty-handed. Patrick was awarded a Winchester rifle by Wells Fargo, and five days later became the youngest deputy U. S. marshal in the territory.

Later that year the marshals learned that the Doolin-Dalton gang was holed up in Ingalls, and they planned their attack. Twelve officers and two civilian wagon drivers would slip into town in two covered wagons as though they were heading for the land rush in the Cherokee Outlet. But when Territorial Governor William Renfrow heard of plans to include the nineteen-year-old deputy, he put his foot down. Patrick couldn't go.

The young man was lucky. The outlaws were warned, and the officers met a fusillade of bullets. Three deputies and two civilians were killed in that shootout.

In 1895 Patrick became a special undercover man for the Santa Fe and Wells Fargo. He rode trains at night, protecting them from outlaws. The night work tired him and he was given two weeks off to rest. He chose to visit an uncle in Deming, New Mexico.

On his way back, he stopped to spend the night in El Paso. It was August 19, his twenty-second birthday, and he entered the Acme saloon for a beer to celebrate.

Patrick, who knew Bill Tilghman, Heck Thomas and other famous lawmen, as well as many of the leading outlaws of the day, recognized John Wesley Hardin, shaking dice at the Acme bar.

Patrick's incredible luck at witnessing famous events continued when old John Selman walked in, put a gun to Hardin's head, and executed one of the worst killers of all time.

Patrick married and moved to Mexico, to become superintendent of construction for the Mexican Central Railway and later a conductor on the line. Then he started writing. But instead of writing from his personal knowledge of the Old West, he wrote four novels set in the east. No publisher was interested.

Then Patrick wrote *Down at Stein's Pass* and *Down at Cross Timbers.* The first, a border drama of New Mexico, had such characters as Geronimo, Billy the Kid, and Pat Garrett. The second, set in the Missouri, had similar kinds of characters. A Boston publisher carried both novels through five printings. They received great reviews throughout the West.

Reviewing *Down at Stein's Pass,* The *San Francisco Call* said, "Opie Reid has met his master," and the *Kansas City Journal* said, "We have read it with pleasure and consider the book a masterpiece." The *Mexican Herald* (Mexico City) said, "*Stein's Pass* embodies much of the Western chivalry the American has learned to love, and in *Cross Timbers* the author pictures his characters a they are, as is proven by the intimacy with which he speaks."

Disappointed in the Mexican Revolution, Patrick moved to San Antonio and wrote another novel, set in the east. Again, no publisher was interested.

He wrote some plays set in Ireland and spent the rest of his working life as a writer, director, and sometime actor in the movies. He never again found the success he had when he wrote what he knew the best. Perhaps he thought his life wasn't interesting enough to write about.

A New York dentist gleaned enough material in a short western vacation to sustain his writing for years. Patrick lived the Old West life and produced only two books. He could have learned something from Zane Grey with his sixty plus novels, which made Grey the most popular writer of his time.

Patrick and Grey were born within two years of each other, started writing the same year, and died within four years of each other. One lived the western life; the other wrote about it.

Suggested reading: Glenn Shirley *Purple Sage* (Stillwater: Barbed Wire Press, 1989).

EXCITING NEWS FROM THE WEST

Wisconsin-born John G. Maher grew up on a Nebraska homestead. After jobs teaching school, delivering mail, and serving as a government land agent, the twenty-eight-year-old was elected county clerk and district court reporter in 1892. He also was a correspondent for the *New York Herald.*

The *Herald* asked its correspondents for lively, even sensational copy, and Maher, its Chadron representative, obliged. Doubting that recently-discovered dinosaur remains in the east were really a million years old, he decided he would produce a million-year-old man.

Maher recruited a six-foot, four-inch cavalryman stationed at nearby Fort Robinson and had him cast in plaster. Then he poured the plaster mold full of concrete. With the help of accomplices — certainly several of them — Maher buried the concrete man near Chadron in the path of a team of fossil-hunting archaeologists.

The scientists reported finding the rare fossil on a rain-collapsed stream bank below twenty-four distinct strata of sedimentary deposits. The man was at least a million years old!

After a co-conspirator had carted the 700-pound treasure around Nebraska for two years, Maher learned that school children were saving pennies to see it. The former school teacher, dismayed at that information, retired the concrete man to a vault in Illinois.

Maher's next inspiration came from the Fenians, an Irish-American Brotherhood determined to overthrow the British government. John O'Neill had once led a raid from New York into Canada, seizing a Canadian village. Then he decided to form a western outpost for the brotherhood, so he brought a group of countrymen to Holt County, Nebraska, and founded the town of O'Neill.

Maher knew the Fenian history, and, in 1895, was ready for his next move. Soon the *Herald* was warning that the British were planning reprisals against the Fenians' violation of Nebraska neutrality. Maher had discovered their plan to steam up the Mississippi, Missouri, and Niobrara Rivers with warships and scatter the Irish patriots. Apparently the New York editors didn't know that Her Majesty's warships would have scraped bottom in the Niobrara, if not before.

The Spanish-American War put the British invasion of Nebraska on the back burner, and Maher enlisted for service in the war. When the war ended, Maher moved to his next big story. He wired the *Herald* that Captain Manuel de Silva Braga, ex-Cuban army officer who happened to be the man who had sunk the USS Maine, had been seen in Chadron. Did they want more on the story?

Did they ever! Public indignation was still high at the mysterious explosion in Havana Harbor which had cost two hundred sixty American lives and brought on a war.

The *Herald* published thrilling eyewitness accounts of dangerous chases which Maher provided, but which unfortunately always just missed their man. Finally, Maher had to manufacture an end for his story.

His creativity rose to the task. He said the international fugitive had been surrounded in an old prospector's cabin up in the Nebraska badlands, and had set it and himself afire. Everything burned up. End of story.

Maher, who had been studying law while exercising his imagination, moved to Lincoln and began law practice.

On the day the United States entered World War One, Maher, aged fifty-three, joined the Army. He rose to the rank of lieutenant colonel.

Later Maher served on the Secretary of War's National Advisory Committee. He became a prominent Nebraska orator and was instrumental in establishing Nebraska's unique unicameral legisature. He also helped organize the American Legion and was Nebraska's first commander of that organization.

Late in Maher's life, Mari Sandoz asked him for some facts related to a book she was writing about her father, Old Jules. Hearing "Old Jules," the experienced story teller was off and running before Sandoz could stop him. Finally, she reminded him that she was Old Jules' daughter and had witnessed the events he was talking about.

Nonplussed, Maher laughed and said, "Well, it was a damn good story the way I was telling it, now wasn't it?"

Apparently John G. Maher had an active mind which needed excitement. What the real world lacked, he provided with his own imagination.

Suggested reading: Nancy M. Peterson, "A Reporter to Match the Wild West" in *True West*, December, 1995.

HE LOVED EXCITEMENT

Rex Beach, born on a Michigan farm, dropped out of college at twenty. He studied law for a few months with his brothers, expecting to practice with them, at least, he thought, until he took his seat on the United States Supreme Court. But law was unexciting, and he followed the gold rush to the Klondike in 1897, still twenty.

Beach spent his first two winters at Rampart City, describing the town as fifteen hundred souls with twelve saloon keepers. "There were no roads or trails," he wrote. "Every valley was a no man's land, every rushing river was a highway to adventure, and every gulch was filled to the brim with a purple haze of mystery."

Beach soon became friends with Frank Canton, famous frontiersman, law officer, and soldier of fortune. He would use him as a prototype for fictional heroes, as did Owen Wister, another Canton friend.

Beach's cabinmate, Canton, described the budding writer as "a handsome young fellow, a husky chap with plenty of backbone and nerve. He could stand up under a pack on the trail as long as any man that I ever met, and he was as good as the best on snowshoes."

During his second winter in the North, Beach bought Canton's cabin from him and rented it for a time to another acquaintance, Wyatt Earp.

Prospecting in the Klondike often took a back seat to simple survival. On one of his journeys to Nome, Beach had to lash his arms to the handlebars of his dog sled. He survived, badly frozen, but one of his Indian guides perished on the trip.

Beach, Canton, and a third partner once set out on a one-hundred-mile journey to the upper reaches of the Tanana River, where they located claims in the Troublesome River Mining District. This trip was marked by a wild dog sled ride when Beach and Canton slid down a mountain slope and almost sailed off into space from a precipice, looming a thousand feet above a canyon. They had topped a ridge above timberline and found a snow-covered trail extending a mile ahead.

Beach challenged Canton to ride the sled down the hill. When Canton accepted, they unhitched the dogs, handed them to their third partner and jumped on the sled, Beach in front. Canton said they were going faster than any express train he had ever seen when he rolled off and yelled to Beach to jump. He got to his feet just in time to see Beach disappear into a snowbank below.

Beach, seeing the danger, had shifted his weight enough to turn the sled. Riding the edge of the precipice, he "struck the soft snowdrift below with such terrific force that the sled tunneled into the snow about thirty feet." Beach crawled out uninjured, "a miraculous escape from death."

Rex Beach's stories of prospecting in the Klondike, a "bleak tundra where God only comes in the spring," made him famous. His sale of "The shyness of Shorty" to *McClure's* launched his career. His first novel, "The Spoilers," brought fame exceeding that of Jack London and Robert W. Service, two other writers of the North.

"The Spoilers" was made into a motion picture four times. Roy Glenister, an honest miner, was played by Gary Cooper in the first sound version (1930). His crooked foe, Alec McNamara, was played by William Boyd, before his Hopalong Cassidy days. Featured in the film was a long fistfight. William Farnum, who played Glenister in the 1914 silent version, was a technical advisor.

Probably the best version of "The Spoilers" was made in 1942 with John Wayne as Glenister and Randolph Scott as McNamara. Marlene Dietrich played the dance-hall queen with some script variance from Beach's novel. The leading roles were played by Jeff Chandler and Rory Calhoun in a 1956 version. Most people remember the long fight between Glenister and McNamara as the highlight of the film.

Including "The Spoilers," thirty of Beach's stories were made into moving pictures.

Beach had a different career for a few weeks in the fall of 1911 when the *New York Times* hired him to cover the world series between the New York Giants and the Philadelphia Athletics. Besides treating readers to a vigorous account of the pitchers' battle between Christy Mathewson of the Giants and Chief Bender of the Athletics, Beach followed his muckraking sentiments to produce what some might say came a half century ahead of its time:

"One leaves the Polo Grounds feeling that baseball is no longer the great American game, but the great American spectacle. Americans no longer play it; they watch it. It is not an athletic pastime; it is a bronchial malady, profiting nobody but the club magnates, the ticket speculators, and the throat specialists."

Sportswriter Grantland Rice said he never saw a man of Beach's brawn who had as much brains as he.

On December 7, 1949, knowing he had inoperable throat cancer, his eyesight failing, and his wife of forty years having recently passed away, Rex Beach killed himself with a shot to the head.

Beach never pretended to psychological depth or philosophical wisdom. He only wanted to entertain. He certainly did that.

Suggested reading: Abe C. Ravitz, *Rex Beach*, (Boise: Boise State University, 1994).

SHE LOVED THE DESERT

I dah Meachem Strobridge survived devastating personal losses to become Nevada's first woman of letters. Her writing career was short — three books published from 1904 to 1909 — but significant.

Idah, an only child, was eight in 1863 when her parents moved from their Moraga Valley, California, ranch to Lassen Meadows, about halfway between present Winnemucca, Nevada, and Lovelock. Her father built a popular hotel for travelers, both those going south across the Forty Mile Desert to the high Sierra crossings and those going west across the Black Rock Desert and the lower crossings to Oregon or down the Lassen Trail to the California gold fields.

Idah soaked up emigrant lore, but she most loved the prospectors, who searched the gray, harsh land for instant riches. She returned to California in 1878 to attend Mills Seminary. When she graduated she married Sam Strobridge and they moved to Lassen Meadows to ranch on land given them by Idah's parents.

Tragedy soon paid its first visit to the young bride. Her first-born son died one day after birth. Shortly after, the 1888-1889 winter killed most of their cattle, and pneumonia took her husband and another son. Her last son died a year later.

Without a husband or children, Idah became manager of her parents' ranch, and started locating mining claims of her own. Soon she had four claims, and she supervised all operations of her four-man crew. But mining didn't pay well, so Idah took up bookbinding and started writing at the age of forty.

Her first book, *In Miners' Mirage Land,* contains powerful writing about the lure, the charm, the beauty of the desert.

"Are you tired of the world's ways?" she asked. "Then if you and the desert have found each other, surely you will feel the drawing of your soul toward the eternal calm — the brooding peace that is there in the gray country."

"How can one convey meaning to another in a language which that other does not understand? I can only tell you the charm of the desert when you, too, have learned to love it. And then there will be no need for me to speak."

Idah recognized that readers might ask, "Is it not a mirage you see — the charm of color and form, and music that you say is in the desert? We do not see these things. We see only uncouth fashioning, where you see magnificence or grace. The cry of the cougar — the coyote's wailing is uncanny to hear; yet you call it music. You tell us there is color in the desert; while we, who know, see nothing but the endless gray."

IDAH MEACHEM STROBRIDGE

Nevada Historical Society

"Well" she answered, "is happiness or beauty or any of the things that give us joy anything more than a mirage? We find in the world only what we, ourselves, bring into it. If we find love, and joy, and beauty, it is because we are capable of loving, and can feel joy, and can see beauty."

Idah's best writing was tied closely to the prospectors she knew and shared campfires with. Old Man Berry, over eighty years old, was a favorite. He was tall and guant and bowed, but not in the back as others of his age. His head was bowed to the ground from fifty years of looking down while he walked, but when he looked up his bright eyes pierced yours like a man half his age.

"There was something royal about the old man," Idah wrote, "and you might join ranch hands and teamsters in good-humored scoffing, but only when his back was turned. No man dared jest ever so lightly to his face. He commanded your respect, and you, too, would have shown him the same deference as they did whenever he spoke."

Idah Strobridge cared little for prospectors who struck it rich and moved to San Francisco or New York or Paris to enjoy their fortune. She would have liked Shorty Harris, a single-blanket jackass prospector in Death Valley. Shorty, who was born two years after Idah and died two years after she did, had found and lost several fortunes, but he never left Death Valley. Late in life Shorty said, "Who in hell wants ten million dollars? It's the game, man — the game."

Idah would have understood. "I doubt if the end of the search would bring joy," she wrote. "To have money in the desert makes little change in one's way of living. And to go to the cities! They are alien to all the cities would give. So, the joy of life for them lies in the search for — not in the finding of gold."

But Idah did move to Los Angeles where she was a neighbor of Mary Hunter Austin, whose book *The Land of Little Rain* resembled Idah's writing. Away from her desert inspiration, Idah's writing dried up. She did continue bookbinding and won first prizes in Alaska and at the California state fair. Maynard Dixon provided some of the illustrations for her books long before he became famous.

Suggested reading, Anthony Amaral, "Idah Meachem Strobridge, First Woman of Nevada Letters," in *Brand Book No. 14, Los Angeles Corral, the Westerners (1974).*

TWO SCOUNDRELS AND A SPUNKY WOMAN

Harry Tammen's mother, widowed when her son was seven, could not care for him. She dressed him in a home-made Dutch suit, several sizes too large, and kissed him goodbye to make his own way in the streets of Philadelphia. The little boy, speaking only German, found work in a beer garden. He grew up in a variety of saloons, but drank very little. By the time he met Frederick Bonfils, he was also in the curio shop business. He sold Geronimo's "genuine scalp" as often as he could find a buyer.

Bonfils, a few years younger than Tammen, grew up with his close relative, Napoleon, back in his native Corsica. After a career of running lotteries, mostly fraudulent and often just one step ahead of the law, he became known as the Napoleon of the Cornfields. During the Oklahoma Land Rush he sold "prime Oklahoma City lots" without telling his mail order buyers they were located in a place called Oklahoma City, Texas.

Tammen was a short, roly-poly man, bubbling with ideas, a born showman, a foe of custom and tradition, a Puck with both hands full of firecrackers. He had practically no formal education.

Bonfils was a lean, athletic man, austere and Spartan in his habits. He watched his bankroll carefully, believing that money brought power and power was God. He had dropped out of West Point to take up his career in lotteries and real estate.

Diametrically opposite in most ways, they had two things in common: both were aggressive fighters, determined to succeed, and neither seemed to have time to grow old in mind or body. In 1895 the scoundrels began a lifetime of business partnerships together, with never a written contract between them. They started out by buying the *Denver Post*, Bonfils putting up the $12,500 capital and Tammen the publishing brains.

"It's a piddling little paper now," Tammen said, "but we'll wean it on tiger milk."

Bonfils refused to put up another cent after the purchase price. Tammen met the first payroll by collecting free railroad passes and selling them to ticket scalpers.

"Harry," Bonfils said happily, "you are a man of foresight and dependability. I predict a great future for the *Denver Post.*"

The newspaper paper attacked public officials, assailed public utilities, reviled its competitors, and blackmailed merchants into paying exorbitant rates for advertising. In this western version of yellow journalism, any *Post* supporter was "prominent," every girl in a romantic news item was "an heiress," every such New York girl was a "Ziegfeld Follies Girl." The subscriber list surged from four thousand to twenty-seven thousand in three years.

Polly Pry, the first woman reporter on the *Post* was beautiful. Born in Virginia, she grew up in a Kentucky horse-raising family, running away at fifteen to marry the president of the Mexican Central Railroad. But tiring of private cars and ambassadorial parties, she went to New York at seventeen, seeking a journalism career. After a stint at *Street & Smith*, where she wrote a short fiction piece once a week, she joined the *Post* in 1898.

At the turn of the century, the *Post* decided to campaign for some things, not just against them. Choosing prison reform, Bonfils and Tammen sent Polly Pry to Cañon City to poke around in the state prison.

There she found Alferd Packer. He had killed and eaten five prospecting companions during a deep snow winter in the San Juan Mountains. Originally convicted of an act that was not a crime when he had his grotesque banquet, Packer was retried, convicted again, and sentenced to life in prison.

"He looked like a nice man," Polly told her bosses. "I know he couldn't have done those horrible things. Why don't you try to get him a pardon?"

Packer had recently been the most talked-about man in Colorado. The judge at his first trial had reportedly said at sentencing: "There was seven Dimmycrats in Hinsdale County, but you, you voracious, man-eating son of a bitch, you done et five of them. I sentence you to be hanged by the neck until you are dead, dead, dead."

The old showman, Tammen, and his shrewd partner, with visions of a traveling one-man circus, hired a lawyer for Packer and began a campaign for a pardon. All they asked of Packer was to be the prize attraction in the circus.

The campaign won a pardon, but not the kind the *Post* owners had in mind. Packer was ordered to not leave the city of Denver! Tammen and Bonfils immediately lost interest, and it took Polly to find the newly-freed man a job as doorman for the *Post.*

The scoundrels' lack of interest extended to W. W. "Plug Hat" Anderson, the attorney they had hired for Packer. They refused to pay the agreed one thousand dollar fee.

To protect himself, Plug Hat took custody of fifteen hundred dollars that Packer had earned in prison by making hair ropes and bridles. When the *Post* owners learned of this perfidy, they hit the ceiling.

"Fire Anderson," Bonfils thundered. "And we won't pay him one cent, either. He's just a damned crook."

"We ought to sic Packer on him," Tammen said.

Polly carried the news to Plug Hat, whose office was just across the street from the *Post.*

POLLY PRY

Denver Public Library
Western History Collection

"Tell your employers I shall call on them at once," Anderson announced.

Polly tried to warn her bosses, but they were sitting peacefully when Anderson entered their office. Tammen immediately began to revile the lawyer.

"Sir," said Anderson, "I am a Missourian and a man of culture."

"You're not a man at all," Tammen shouted. "You're a low down son of a bitch! And a robber to boot."

Anderson's face turned white and he reached into his overcoat pocket.

"Look out," Polly screamed. "He's got a gun."

Bonfils lunged at Anderson, knocking him down before he could get the gun out. He jumped on top of the lawyer and was ready to beat him to death when Polly intervened.

"Don't, Fred," she implored. "It will be a terrific scandal. Let him go."

Bonfils stepped back and a very groggy lawyer, his face bleeding, got to his feet.

"Now get out, you bastardly thief," Bonfils ordered.

As Anderson staggered toward the door, Tammen determined to get his licks in. He gave the departing lawyer the best billingsgate he had distilled from a lifetime of chicanery and yellow journalism.

But Plug Hat Anderson didn't stay departed long. After Bonfils pushed him out, the door suddenly swung back, a gun appeared, and the three occupants of the room could see Anderson's eyes, gleaming over the barrel.

"Look out," Polly screamed.

Plug Hat's first bullet hit Bonfils, ploughing through his shoulder into his throat. Tammen dived behind a table between the partners' desks, cursing and howling, thinking Bonfils had been killed. Plug Hat snarled as he turned his gun on Tammen and shot him twice, once in the wrist, once in the shoulder.

Polly realized that any defense would have to come from her. She jumped over to Tammen, hiding him beneath her skirts, and she struggled with Plug Hat for the gun. The barrel was hot, but she hung on bravely as Tammen's blood stained her dress. Staff members heard the screams and the shots, but stood outside the door, paralyzed, as the spunky Virginia woman fought her lone battle against the gentleman from Missouri.

Plug Hat, still struggling with Polly for the gun, threatened to kill her.

"Go ahead," she said, calmly. "Then you'll really hang."

By now Bonfils was unconscious, barely breathing, and Tammen was still under Polly's skirts. Two men out in the street had heard the screams and were entering the building. But Plug Hat, coming to his senses, told Polly he was through, and he left the room, gun in his pocket.

Anderson walked past the *Post* employees, and went immediately to the Police station. He handed his gun to the sergeant, saying, "I just killed two snakes named Bonfils and Tammen. Put me under arrest."

But they didn't die. When the surgeon started to remove Tammen's shirt, the wounded man protested, saying, "Don't cut it, damn it, it's silk."

Bonfils might have died if he hadn't had an enormous will to live. He had nightmares for the rest of his life and kept a man near to awaken him when they came in his sleep. He carried one bullet to his grave.

Bonfils' throat had been so affected from his wound he could never smoke again. He loved tobacco, and one of the bizarre sights at the *Post* after the shooting was watching this relative of Napoleon sit calmly, while an employee blew cigarette smoke in his face.

Anderson was cleared of all charges. It is claimed that during his trial he got a bouquet and a note from the Governor. The note read: "I congratulate you on your intention, but must condemn your poor aim."

Bonfils never forgave Polly Pry for saving his life. She had done something for him that he could not do for himself. The obligation, for him, was abhorrent to his defiant nature. He picked quarrels with her and often accused her of lying.

A woman who wrestles with a smoking gun doesn't take that lightly. Polly left the *Post* and continued with her literary career. Her tenderness toward Packer had been misplaced, but her courage had known no bounds.

Polly survived an assassination attempt in 1904, and tried to become a war correspondent in World War One. She had to settle for an assignment as public relations officer for the Red Cross in the Balkans.

She died in 1939, aged eighty.

Suggested reading: Gene Fowler, *Timber Line* (New York: Blue Ribbon Books, 1933.)

ORDERING INFORMATION

True Tales of the Old West
is projected for 40 volumes.

For Titles in Print —
Ask at your bookstore
or write:

PIONEER PRESS
P. O. Box 216
Carson City, NV 89702-0216
(775) 888-9867
FAX (775) 888-0908

Other titles in progress include:

Pioneer Children	Frontier Courts & Lawyers
Old West Riverboaters	Frontier Artists
Army Women	Californios
Western Duelists	Early West Explorers
Government Leaders	Homesteaders
Early Lumbermen	Old West Merchants
Frontier Militiamen	Scientists & Engineers
Preachers & Spirit Guides	Frontier Teachers
Teamsters & Packers	Visitors to the Frontier
Doctors & Healers	Storms & Floods
Mysteries & Ghosts	Wild Animals